Bhimsen Joshi, My Father

Bhimsen Joshi in 1962, Pune

Raghavendra Bhimsen Joshi

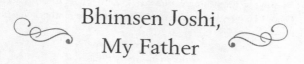

Bhimsen Joshi, My Father

Translated from Marathi by Shirish Chindhade

OXFORD
UNIVERSITY PRESS

OXFORD
UNIVERSITY PRESS

Oxford University Press is a department of the University of Oxford.
It furthers the University's objective of excellence in research, scholarship,
and education by publishing worldwide. Oxford is a registered trademark of
Oxford University Press in the UK and in certain other countries

Published in India by
Oxford University Press
YMCA Library Building, 1 Jai Singh Road, New Delhi 110001, India

© Oxford University Press 2016

First published in Marathi by Shabd Publication in 2013
First English translation published by Oxford University Press in 2016

ISBN-13: 978-0-19-946711-2
ISBN-10: 0-19-946711-0

Typeset in Garamond LT Std 12/15.5
by Tranistics Data Technologies, Kolkata 700091
Printed in India by Replika Press Pvt. Ltd

All photographs appearing in the book are from the author's personal collection

To my mother who stood like a rock to protect and groom us
To my wife who has held my hand at every moment of my life
To the divine notes of my father Bhimsen Joshi, to which
I am always tied through my umbilical cord

From the Heart

I UTTER THE WORDS 'Bhimsen Joshi's son' and I see the images of Swarbhaskar Bhimanna flash through the minds of those around me. It is, indeed, a rare fortune to be born to a celebrity and also to be a sensitive person who is aware of it. Many have written about Bhimanna's greatness. Even so, it is good to understand his greatness through his music rather than through descriptive words. I saw, touched, and worshipped both his personas—the ordinary man and the genius. He appealed to me equally intensely as a human being and through his music, both being clear and immaculate. He accepted full responsibility for everything he did in his life and gave expression to his suffering through his music.

When two minds unite, they converse without words. They resonate like two tanpuras playing in unison. That was precisely how I connected with Bhimanna: I received and understood him through his music. So what if some called it father-worship!

The halo around a celebrity often eclipses those around him and relegates them to the dark wings of a stage from where they can only watch him. They live out their lives in darkness as mere witnesses to a privileged being.

I am content with the ordinariness that enabled me to understand and appreciate Bhimanna's extraordinariness. Sometimes when I wake up in the early hours of the morning,

1

I tuck myself into the tent of my quilt and hold close to me scenes from days gone by. A retake of those days flashes across my mind, and I am amazed by the creativity of the great director of the movie called Life.

Does life mean a mere exchange of millions of messages between the mind and the body through nerves connecting the brain and the spinal cord? Why do some cages, that we call Body, hold such sensitive souls? What inspires the sunflower to follow the sun? Why do some flowers keep vigil through the night for the brilliance of daybreak? It was one such moment of heightened consciousness that inspired me to write this book. That is how this book was born. It contains nothing but the bare truth.

One

ONE NIGHT IN NAGPUR, when I was about six years old, I was rudely woken up by my mother's loud wailing. 'I'm undone! Ruined!'

My two sisters were fast asleep. Mother had stuffed the end of her sari into her mouth and was crying violently. I got up, poured a glass of water for her, and gently patted her back to calm her down. Though still a child, in that instant I matured suddenly.

Only a couple of days earlier, Bhimanna—Bhimsen Joshi, my father, the great Hindustani classical vocalist—had brought me and my sister Usha here from Gadag in Karnataka, and had himself immediately proceeded to Poona. My mother along with my other sister Sumangala had already reached Nagpur.

I recalled an evening in Gadag a week earlier. I was playing with Damodar, my step-uncle. Suddenly a quarrel broke out between us which led to a fight. I was punching him left and right when he, too, lost his temper and overpowered me. I began to howl. Madhukaka, my uncle, who was watching us, came to my rescue. He held Damodar's hand and snapped, 'Don't you understand that his parents are not here? Why are you beating him?' I realized then that things were not really right with us.

Another recollection is of being in a dark compartment of a train. The windows had been pulled down as it was raining hard. As I tried to look through the glass pane, I had a premonition of some impending danger. I was going to Nagpur with Bhimanna. My mother and my newborn sister, Sumangala, had already left for Nagpur with Mahashabde, a neighbour from Gadag. My younger sister Usha and I were going to join them.

I also remember the interim stay in Poona when we had stayed with the family of the 'other woman' in the Awate tenement. It consisted of a long, narrow row of rooms in an old house. 'Her' mother was resting on the cot outside. I remember her as being short, fat, and fair. Her forehead bore no red mark. Her sisters fondly addressed Bhimanna as 'Mr Joshi'. A brother who loitered around was called 'Appa' by Bhimanna. I was too young to understand the situation. Later on, I learnt that their debt-ridden father was dead, leaving behind this hungry family. All these youngsters depended on her and, in due course of time, she got all of them married and settled. It was at this point in our lives that she succeeded in entrapping Bhimanna.

It was only when I grew up that I got to know from my mother, Sunanda, why we had been packed off to Nagpur. From the family elders I learnt the story of Bhimanna and my mother. They were cousins and had known each other since childhood. He often visited Atchutacharya Katti, his maternal uncle, at Badami in Karnataka. He was a favourite of his uncle's, who was fond of music and singing, and this formed a bond between the two. They would put together a few silver rupee coins, mount their horses, and go to a nearby place to gamble. Bhimanna once told me, to my surprise, that his uncle sometimes gave him money, which he would spend on food.

Bhimanna was a regular annual visitor to Badami during the festival of Guddad Ranga, Krishna of the Mountains, the family deity of the Kattis. An elaborate puja used to be performed in the month of Kartik, which Bhimanna would attend along with friends from Gadag. Among them was Vyankanna the wrestler, who could easily bend a steel rod. Years later, he became an expert bonesetter.

Rammama, my mother's cousin, once gave me a good description of the temple where the puja was performed. Situated a couple of miles away from Badami, it was an ancient temple built by a king, and was flanked by mountains on three sides. On the right there was a large, open space and a sprawling yard. On the left, a little tucked away between the mountain crags, there was a sweet-water stream and a tank from which devotees would carry back holy water while returning from their pilgrimage. The architectural sites of Aihole and Pattadakallu, famous worldwide, are situated nearby.

After the puja, they would sit down to listen to Bhimanna's bhajans. Rammama recalled that he first heard Mahipati Dasa's bhajan '*Yanna paliso karunakara*' (O God, be compassionate to me) rendered by Bhimanna at one such performance.

Bhimanna would enjoy the sumptuous meals and festivities with his friends and relatives from his mother's side of the family. Sweets were usually forced on the guests, and Bhimanna could polish off a whole plateful of laddus with ease; but he soon gave up the habit of eating too many sweets. Mother too used to talk of the Badami days. Situated by the side of a lake, Badami boasted of several cave carvings and ancient temples, including a beautiful temple of Goddess Banshankari. She told us how they used to play in the sweet-water stream of Saraswati. The spacious tank in the precincts of the temple is proof of its ancient glory.

It was in this beautiful Badami that my mother and Bhimanna came together and where, subsequently, Alaknanda Katti became Mrs Sunanda Bhimsen Joshi.

The Kattis were a prestigious family of Badami, and the father, Atchutacharya, was an important person in the town. He owned vast properties of land and, as Bhimanna once told me, his annual income was well over a hundred thousand rupees. When he was implicated in a court litigation, he paid his lawyer, the reputed barrister Mohammed Ali Jinnah, a thousand rupees for one appearance. Sunanda was fourth in line after her sisters Kamala, Prema, and Shamala. She was only eleven months old when she lost her mother and, initially for a few days, she was looked after by Atchutacharya's mistress. Later, she was brought up by her elder sisters. Sunanda was beautiful and of fair complexion, and had prominent eyes and a round face. Her black hair reached down to her ankles. Her elder sister, Kamala, who lived in Badami, took charge of Sunanda's schooling. Sunanda did well at school and completed her finals. She was well-groomed in the orthodox ways of Brahmins. She observed all fasts devoutly, recited Kannada bhajans and prayers, and knew many devotional songs of Purandara Dasa. All these traditional treasures were further polished with her visits to the temple.

Atchutacharya Katti acted on the stage, sometimes with Sunanda sitting on his back. Once when he was playing the serious role of Dhritarashtra of Mahabharata, Sunanda got scared and began to cry. This short-tempered man simply threw her off, and she hurt her left hand, which never functioned properly later in life. Nevertheless, her good looks more than made up for her minor disability. But, this act of being flung away was a forewarning: rejection by her own people in future and that too for no fault of hers.

At the age of thirteen, Sunanda was placed in the care of her elder sister Premakka Hungund in Dharwad. Although their father had passed away by then, back in those days it was considered a family duty to look after children without parents. A couple of years later she came back to Badami to stay in the care of another elder sister, Kamala.

By now Sunanda was sixteen and of a marriageable age, according to the established practice in those days; and her maternal aunt's son, Bhimsen, was twenty-one. Initially, the name of the elder Shamala was to be proposed to him, but she declared that she did not want to marry someone constantly on the move with a tanpura. A biographer of Bhimsen's once told me that Sunanda, too, had been unwilling to enter into this alliance. This is, however, only a piece of twisted, false propaganda. Bhimanna's mother Ramabai wished to get him married to her brother's daughter. However, his father Guracharya Joshi was a bit doubtful about the economic status of the Katti family, addicted as they were to gambling and betting. Ramabai went on a hunger strike to put pressure on him, but Guracharya was also aware of the fact that an ordinary singer stood little chance of an alliance with a prestigious family. Bhimanna, who occasionally met Sunanda, once gifted her with face cream, talcum powder, and a blouse-piece with a request, 'Nandi, marry me. Don't say no.'

My aunts teased her to no end over this episode. Sunanda was in the prime of her youth and was a desirable match for anyone who wanted to marry her. So the alliance was sealed and the ceremony of exchanging rings was held.

While talks for Bhimanna's marriage were in progress, his father Guracharya received a letter in Marathi written by a young girl. Since Ramabai had lived with Guracharya in Pandharpur, in Maharashtra, for long, she knew Marathi well. She read out the letter to him, which was to the effect that a young girl had expressed her desire to marry Bhimanna. This was quite a bold step as, in those days, it was the elders who arranged the marriage of the young. However, this helped expedite the marriage talks for Bhimanna. When Guracharya asked for an explanation, Bhimanna said, 'There is no love affair. Nothing of the sort whatsoever. I met this girl at the Hyderabad radio station. That's all.' I thought that Bhimanna, who had left home in childhood for the love of music, in search of a guru, could have easily given it up for love again. My own teacher Prahladbuwa Joshi once told me that he, too, had received a similar letter in his youth. Sunanda's elder sister Kamala's mother-in-law, Subhadramma Sodegar, volunteered to defray the wedding expenses while the sisters took care of other details. Under these circumstances the wedding took place.

All relatives lived nearby, but Bhimanna went personally to Bombay to invite his close friends Jalihal, Narahari Kulkarni, and the radio artists. He requested his younger brother Narayan to accompany him who, however, asked, 'Why do you need me?' Bhimanna asked shyly, 'You want me to go around inviting people to my own wedding?' He had a clean and sensitive nature.

The wedding took place in 1944. Bhimanna along with his friends raised the pandal. That was how our grandfather managed his finances! His younger brother Vyankateshkaka told me that Bhimanna refused to ride a horse during the wedding procession. Bhimanna particularly invited his *gurubhagini*, Gangubai Hangal, who attended the function with her daughter Krishna. Krishna and Bhimanna's younger sister Hema were the *karwali*, holding the water pots behind the bride and the groom. Hema Aunty herself told me that a photographer had been booked, but he was sent away as no one was willing to pay him. Alas! Not a single photograph of Bhimanna's mother Ramabai is available. Guracharya has written the following account of the wedding in his book *Nadedu Band Dare*:[1]

Got Bhimsen married in 1944. This put him into a disciplined household routine. Although a number of people thought that the marriage had been a hasty decision, he and I were aware of his inner needs. We are convinced, even today, that his burgeoning youth needed to be anchored in a marriage. It would have been an added advantage if his wife too had been well versed in music. But, it goes without saying that this marriage certainly strengthened his concentration and added vigour and depth to his music.

Those who claim that they shaped and made Bhimsen were well aware that he was a mature artist even before they knew him. Bhimanna's first radio performance was broadcast by Radio Lucknow in 1939. His mother heard this on the radio at the nearby Shinappa's Hotel. In 1944, HMV produced his first recorded disc. Bhimanna played it for his mother on a gramophone borrowed from an acquaintance. Narayankaka was a witness to this episode.

Soon after his wedding, Bhimanna's sister Hema visited a neighbour in Gadag. The women of the house asked her, 'Tell us how your brother was able to win such a charming wife. Did he abduct her?' Poor little Hema wept on her mother's shoulder. That was how Bhimanna was looked upon by others since he did nothing—except sing!

Bhimanna used to give singing lessons to a doctor's wife, partly to earn some money and partly because of Guracharya's pressure. The doctor agreed since his wife was fond of music. However, when it came to paying Bhimanna's fees, the doctor was always reluctant. He believed that music was a useless art in the world of respectable people. Bhimanna got into an argument with him. The quarrel reached the ears of Guracharya who supported the doctor. An angry Bhimanna vowed never again to give private tuition in music to anyone.

Music has no importance in the world of those who think that education is the only means of earning money. They have no love for it. In the course of time, a number of doctors and engineers became Bhimanna's friends. Many of them admitted to him that anyone with a bit of hard work and rote-learning could become an engineer or a doctor, but music and singing could not be learnt this way: it requires exceptional imagination and talent. Doctors and engineers could also achieve it if they possessed imagination and talent. On the other hand, there are scores of engineers who may not be able to tell a spanner from a screwdriver!

Ramabai, Bhimanna's mother, died of postpartum disorder soon after her son's wedding. Bhimanna was so perturbed by the news that he avoided his father for a long time after her death. But some days later, when they happened to pass each other by chance, they embraced and wept bitterly. Inscrutable are the ways of destiny, after all. During the Second World War, Guracharya had wished to join the defence services. He was an MA and could have easily walked off with a good offer. However, the war ended and his dreams were shattered. Had our grandmother lived longer, all the bitterness that later pervaded our lives might never have crept in.

Bhimanna's younger sister, Vanamala, had married into the Deshpande family of Bagalkot. His brothers Narayan and Vyankatesh, having matriculated, were on the threshold of college education. Madhav, Hema, and Madhu, the youngest three, were still at school. A short time after his wife's death, Guracharya decided to remarry. After all, there had to be a woman in the house to look after the children. This was the beginning of a new episode in our lives.

Grandfather was about fifty and quite healthy. Both for his own sake and for his children's, he married Godabai of Ningdhalli. A fortnight after the wedding, Godabai's brother Balbhimanna came wielding a cudgel and throwing out a challenge for grandfather to come out to fight. His anger was justified as during the marriage negotiations Guracharya had mentioned only his three young children, not the grown-up sons and daughters! On the other hand, Godabai had reached spinsterhood. Since both parties needed each other, the situation was solved satisfactorily.

When Godabai came to her new home, she bent before Bhimanna to pay him due respect, but he stopped her and said, 'I am your eldest son'. She was younger than him in age. There was a lot of stress in the house: Guracharya found it difficult to provide for such a large family. He wanted Narayan and Vyankatesh to work after their matriculation, but Guracharya's brothers were against discontinuing their education. The atmosphere at home was deeply traditional, and everybody had to follow rules meticulously. In an interview with Sahyadri TV channel, Bhimanna told the critic Ashok Ranade that he was paid higher rates than most of his contemporaries, but all earnings had to be handed over to his father.

My mother often recalled many incidents of those times. Once when Bhimanna returned from a concert, he saw my mother—his wife—in wet clothes, drawing water from the well in the yard for home consumption, a common chore in many households. Guracharya had rented out rooms in our house to some young students who used to move around freely in the yard. Bhimanna, furious, shouted at her, 'Get back into the house this minute!' And he told his father, 'My wife will not do such work anymore. Make other arrangements.'

Bhimanna was non-committal about his father's remarriage, but his younger brother Narayan did not approve of it. After all, they belonged to different age groups. Guracharya's brothers led similar lives: after the death of their first wives with whom they had had several children, they remarried and had even more children! Guracharya was criticized in the local newspapers for his second marriage, but he boldly replied, 'I am hale and hearty. There has to be a woman in the house to look after the children. Besides, I have helped a spinster to enjoy the pleasure of having her own household.' In those times, many men looked for pleasure outside marriage in the beds of their mistresses. Guracharya abstained from this. My mother told me that he fathered nine children from the second marriage. Godabai, the stepmother, looked after all the children from Guracharya's first marriage as well as my mother with loving care and diligence. Whenever Guracharya was away preaching, the two women took the chance to order spicy dishes from a hotel and enjoy them over a cup of tea, Godaajji told me.

One day Guracharya asked Bhimanna to set up a separate residence and also look after his two brothers, Narayan and Vyankatesh. This was a bolt from the blue as Bhimanna was not yet earning a regular income.

I was born around this time, on 26 July 1945. My mother had been taken for delivery to Dr Umachgi's dispensary the previous night. But she had not delivered till morning when Bhimanna had to catch a train for a performance in a different town. I was born soon after the train departed. When my father returned a few days later, he went directly to my mother's room, caressed her face, and said, 'You have repaid my debt by giving me a son'. In those days in Karnataka it was regarded a matter of great luck to have a son as the firstborn.

Bhimanna himself was the first son in the family. Within six months of my birth, Godabai, our step-grandmother, gave birth to Damodar.

Bhimanna rented a house in Dharwad as many of our relatives lived near Gadag. Narayan and Vyankatesh were enrolled in college. Narayan even got some fee relief, thanks to a professor's love for Bhimanna's singing. Narayan told me that Bhimanna and my mother looked after them with loving care for a couple of years. Mother even sold her gold to pay the fees.

The atmosphere at home used to be jolly and we would often exchange jokes and playful banter. Bhimanna had had a new jacket stitched for a performance. When the programme was over, he handed it over to Narayan saying, 'You should have it now. There are girls in your college!' Bhimanna knew that Narayan had a crush on a girl in his college. Vyankatesh was a science student. I was their favourite. They addressed my father as 'Bhimanna', elder brother. I, too, used the same word to address him. The two addressed my mother as 'Vahini', sister-in-law; hence I, too, started calling her that. We lived in Dharwad even after the birth of my sister Usha. We had our photographs taken at the studio. In my solo photograph, I looked quite dapper. When my grandfather saw it, he exclaimed, 'A chip of the old block!' Indeed I resembled Bhimanna a great deal.

Bhimanna would sit under the tree in front of the house and practice singing round the clock. A servant in the neighbouring house wondered what work Bhimanna did for a living. Years later, when television reached homes, Bhimanna's concert was telecast. The mistress of the house called the servant and asked him to identify the singer on the screen. 'Do you see who this person is?' she asked. When the man failed to identify him, the lady said, 'This is Bhimsen Joshi, the man you used to see singing under the tree!' The man saluted the TV and exclaimed, 'God! How great he has grown!'

After I was married, my mother would recall many a story. Once when Bhimanna had just returned after giving a recital, he felt that the atmosphere in the house was a little too subdued. On inquiring what the matter was, he was told that the family was in mourning because a relative from my father's side had passed away. Bhimanna had brought back a basket full of fresh golden marigolds. In those days, it was considered a sign of disrespect to talk to one's wife in the presence of elders. Despite that, he took my mother aside, placed the basket in her hands, and said, 'We have scores of relations in the Joshi family. If you observe mourning for each and every one of them, the whole year will be a time of mourning. Wear these flowers in your hair when you come to the bedroom at night.' My mother found herself caught between Scylla and Charybdis. If she were seen with flowers in her hair, she was sure to be chided; if she did not wear them, Bhimanna would be furious! 'But I managed it somehow,' said my mother to my wife. Fresh flowers for her long, dark, ankle-length hair was, after all, Bhimanna's way of appreciating her beauty!

Once my mother's elder sister Kamakka of Badami invited her to celebrate *mangala-gour* festivities, the ritualistic pooja with song and dance offered to Goddess Gouri on a Tuesday by newly married girls. Gadag, near Badami, was only a day's journey away, but Bhimanna wouldn't allow her to go. Finally he consented on the condition that she would be back by the same night. Once the puja and all the festivities were over, my mother was preparing to return, but it started raining heavily. She just could not reach the railway station—all the roads were waterlogged. Her sister comforted her, promising her to apprise Bhimanna of the situation.

At about three in the morning, there was heavy banging on the door. Smeared in mud from top to toe, Bhimanna stood at the door with his bicycle resting on his shoulders! The muddy roads had prevented him from riding it. 'Didn't I tell you I cannot stay away from you even for one night? Why did you stay over?' Kamakka let them have the privacy of a room and the man cooled down. Even in her old age my mother derived deep solace from such memories.

By now Narayan and Vyankatesh had graduated and left for Banaras and Bombay, respectively, for higher education. Soon the vacuum was filled in by Shamacharya, the harmonium accompanist, and Rotti Shinappa, the tabla player. Mother cooked for them as well. At that time, Bhimanna shifted residence to Badami, his maternal uncle's place. Everybody knew him and he was familiar with the place. Kamakka lived there, too, and kept my mother company whenever Bhimanna was away giving recitals. His practising meant a continuous exercise for the family as the accompanists stayed with us. Sometimes he even chose to practise to his heart's content in the Guddad Ranga temple.

Once I asked Bhimanna about the ambience there and he fell into a reverie, recollecting happy memories of the days when peace had come gently like dewdrops and Bhimanna could work on the bass and volume of his voice. 'I was free to sing as loudly as I wished. No one would be disturbed,' he said. And, of course, his music-loving friends always accompanied him everywhere. Who would miss such a rare treat? One of his better-off friends always ensured a steady supply of tobacco, paan-supari (betel leaves and betel nut), and a lot of tasty *chivda* (a spicy snack). Later on, after many years had passed, Bhimanna happened to drive to Badami in his car and saw his old friend in tatters in the market square. He was so moved that he stopped the car, got down, and embraced his old pal, to the great amazement of those around. It was like Lord Krishna embracing Sudama, his destitute childhood mate! Bhimanna bought him a set of new clothes and also gave him some money to repay him for his tasty chivda of the old days.

Mother often got lost in memories of the happy days spent in Badami. She could not resist the urge to share them with my wife. She would invariably declare that in those days the vegetables and the food had a unique taste and flavour. She regularly bought a pot of fresh homemade butter to go with the *bhakri* (jowar roti). 'Even then he would make me pour a ladleful of *tadka* [seasoning in hot oil] over it,' she recalled. He was especially fond of *muddipalya*, a dish made of fenugreek leaves and lentils. There was no dearth of milk; tea had to be served a dozen times during his practice sessions. It was, as the old adage goes, 'A married woman must never say no to vermilion, nor a man to tea!'

Bhimanna practised the lower notes, the *kharja*, only early in the morning. Once after drinking a cup of tea, he tried his bass practice, but failed to touch the low notes even after repeatedly clearing his throat. Another cup of tea was ordered, and as he put the saucer to his mouth, he heard a calf bellowing in the yard. Instantly he put down the saucer, shouted, 'This is genuine kharja!' and started practising it.

I, too, have a few faint memories of the days in Badami. Once I was playing with a coconut ring traditionally made for a particular festival. Suddenly a monkey came out of the blue and snatched it away. I began to cry and was taken ill. I cannot remember without terror the hypodermic needle the doctor injected me with. The very sight of an injection syringe frightens me even today.

Mother told me that when Bhimanna had typhoid he was bedridden for a long time. His body temperature often fluctuated to alarming degrees. Thanks to the local doctor's treatment and Mother's vigilant care, he recuperated slowly. However, one day he ran such a high temperature that he became delirious. She rubbed some salt over his head, a popular home remedy. He had almost lost his voice then. However, after a month, he drank a cup of good strong tea, tried to sing, and found his voice again. He shouted out to Mother, 'Nandi, I got my voice back again!' He recovered steadily thereafter and started to sing again. Though a wife is expected to render such services in caring for her husband, I believe that my mother's love and devoted care contributed greatly to the rebirth of this god of music, the future Bharat Ratna.

Bhimanna's uncles, Govindkaka and Ramkaka, once staged a Kannada play called *Bhagyashree*. Lakshamrao Bendre had written it especially for Bhimanna. Ramkaka was a veteran actor and had been honoured by the government. He had a 'soft corner' for female artists. Though Bhimanna was to perform the main role, the crux of the matter was who would play the heroine's part. In those days, women did not usually act in plays. However, Bhimanna knew a girl named Vatsala Mudholkar of Aurangabad, in Maharashtra, whom he had met at a radio station. She performed in travelling theatres across the state and was used to staying with people in different places. She had been tutored in music in Jalna by 'prestigious' teachers. Although she did not have even a smattering of Kannada, she was invited to Dharwad as the female lead in the play. She came into close contact with Bhimanna who trained her in delivering the Kannada dialogues of the play. Ramkaka had no objection to such intimacies. He followed the one-night-stand policy and did not think much about it. Finally the play was performed in Dharwad, Bombay, and Poona. The performances over, Bhimanna returned to Badami for his music practice and to his wife and home.

No one, least of all my mother, had the slightest inkling that the play *Bhagyashree* would ruin Bhimanna's family life. In later years, whenever my mother recalled the entire episode, she cursed in the foulest terms the part played by Ramkaka and the other Joshi elders in the tragedy. What else could this poor, weak woman have done after all!

One day 'that' woman arrived in Badami and fell at my mother's feet, crying and assuring her that 'she' had come to be Bhimanna's student and would continue to be only that. My mother was easily deceived. She was pregnant for the third time, after me and Usha. The woman settled herself in one of the rooms owned by my mother's sister, who lived close by. Occasionally, my mother or her sister even sent 'her' food.

A couple of months after my sister Sumangala's birth, Bhimanna disappeared. It was the darkest day in my mother's life. The bag containing precious articles was open and her gold chain was missing. She cooked as usual and waited for Bhimanna to come back for lunch, but there was no sign of him. That very moment my mother's niece Sudha rushed in to say that 'that woman' too had disappeared! Bhimanna had mentioned to a friend that he was scheduled to perform at the Nagpur radio station. The lovers had headed there. My mother's accouchement had rendered her helpless with no support whatsoever from her parents or her in-laws. She was paralysed with fear. She wept all the way to the family guru, Raghavendra Swami, in Mantralayam. Usha and I were sent away to our grandparents in Gadag. Mother left baby Sumangala in a niche in the temple and, clad in wet clothes with tears streaming from her eyes, performed a rigorous prayer and penance.

The swami's advice was clearly understood by her heart: *Under no circumstances give up hope. Do not think of separating from your husband. Do not buckle down in the face of difficulties.* Her sisters advised her to follow Bhimanna resolutely. She often had suicidal thoughts, but the thought of the three of us prevented her from such rashness. Eventually my mother went to Nagpur with Sumangala, and Bhimanna came to Gadag and took Usha and me with him to Nagpur. That was in 1951.

Shamakka, my maternal aunt, warned Bhimanna, 'You may behave waywardly now, but this second house of yours will never last'. She was a righteous and a god-fearing woman and her words had a prophetic ring. (In later years, Bhimanna had to suffer ill treatment at the hands of 'her' and her people.)

'She' soon saw that her immoral alliance was too flagrant to be sanctioned by Nagpur society, especially in view of Bhimanna's young wife burdened with three children. 'She' moved to Poona with Bhimanna where they were not known by many. The writer of the book *Bhimsen*, at 'her' insistence, claimed that Shrimant Baburao Deshmukh endorsed the second marriage. In fact, he gave a piece of his mind to Bhimanna for such indiscretion. 'She' spread stories about Bhimanna's first wife being mentally weak. Several ill-wishers, too, spread the canard—a striking instance of fabrication and falsehood! Even Goebbels would have admired the level of this propaganda. However, reality would dawn when people met my mother and saw us, Bhimanna's three children.

Even so, Mother's missing gold chain had now been forged into a *mangalsutra*, the auspicious thread that hung around 'her' neck—the alliance having been consummated with the offering of a Satyanarayan puja. Although the puja was a family practice with the Joshis, my mother gave it up for good.

I have distinct memories of the Nagpur stay. We had rented an apartment, located near the Shukrawar Tank, in a house owned by Mr Thakur. The Thakur couple was full of affection for us and an unfailing support to my mother. Janatai Thakur was like a second mother and often fed us sweet curds. She would take us to wedding parties where we enjoyed bhaji-rice. The beastly Nagpur summer hardly bothered us in such kind care. Mother used to send me out to buy a garland for the swami every Thursday from a stall near the temple. Once after returning home, I found Mother was not there. I ran like mad through the market streets looking for her, so out of my mind that a horse carriage ran me down. I escaped almost unscathed except for a few bruises on my body.

I also recall the delicious food served in silver plates at the banquet hosted by Shrimant Deshmukh on the bullock festival day, the *hurda* (roasted and spiced jowar) party held at his farm, and many more such pleasures. We used to sleep on the terrace, in the cool clear night, under a star-studded sky, and I often crooned the popular Hindi film song, '*Awara hoon ... asman ka tara hoon*' (I am a wanderer, a lonely star in the skies).

Mother had been brought up in the conservative Kannadiga upbringing. I had done my first form in the Kannada medium and was now enrolled in a Marathi-medium school. During her three days of menstrual isolation, Mother usually asked me to cook at home. Sometimes just outside the window above the hearth, I would spot a couple of mongooses playfully running around; I enjoyed watching them. After a year in Nagpur we moved to Poona.

Soon after my examination was over, Vyankanna—Bhimanna's brother Vyankatesh—came to take us all to Poona. Mother prepared laddus and chivda for the journey. There was nothing much to be packed, only a stove, a few pots and pans, and a brightly burnished bronze pitcher. Janatai gave us many useful gadgets. I packed a bronze squirt, a gift to me from Janatai.

While packing up, Mother was depressed. She would often weep silently. After the trauma in Badami we had settled down comfortably in Nagpur among loving friends. Initially she had been a little confused in the new atmosphere, surrounded by strangers and having to learn a new language. It was Janatai who had helped her to recover with loving care, help, and consolatory counselling. Mother was overwhelmed with such goodness. My schoolmates, who used to frequent our house, promised to remember us after we were gone. Among them was my best friend, Dilip Badve.

The day of departure dawned. We fell at the feet of the Thakur couple. My mother broke down in uncontrollable sobs.

'Janatai, what is going to happen to me and my children now? Who will be my help and succour?' she sobbed.

'Sunanda,' consoled Janatai, 'have courage. Live for your lovely children. Tough times don't last. God is great. Things change for the better....' Janatai then hugged my mother and gently pushed a currency note into her hand.

We cast a last lingering glance at the house that had sheltered us so lovingly and left with Vyankanna. The horse carriage was waiting outside.

We never went back to Nagpur. But whenever it is mentioned, Janatai and her robust husband flash before my mind's eye with their affectionate, smiling faces. My mother remembers them as God Vithoba and his wife Rakhumai.

~

1.   Gururaj B. Joshi, 'Bhimsen Joshi', in *Nadedu Band Dare* (The Path Traversed), vol. 3 (Dharwad: Manohar Grantha Mala, 1961), p. 2430. The article was subsequently published as *Tandey Kannaninde Pandit Bhimsen Joshi* (Pandit Bhimsen Joshi in the Eyes of His Father) (Dharwad: Manohar Grantha Mala: 2011).

Two

'IT'S POONA STATION. GET DOWN. Poona station.' The sounds around woke me up. Vyankanna said, 'Come, Raghappa, this is Poona. We are getting down here.' The sprawling crowded station scared me for a while. Vyankanna made us sit on a bench and went somewhere. When he returned, he took us to a huge building. I had learnt to read Marathi and saw a board with 'Gokuldas Dharmashala' written on it. It was a rest house, a charity home.

A room on the upper floor was allotted to us rent-free. Vyankanna was still a student and was not well-off. After washing up at the common tap, Mother took out the tiffin carrier containing laddus and chivda which we had for breakfast. Tea and milk were ordered from a restaurant on the ground floor. This done, Vyankanna left again.

I was busy observing from the window the movement of the crowds on the station road. Vyankanna returned after a long while and brought us lunch. Mother was restless. 'Brother, what is happening? Did you meet *him* or not? What did he say?' She fired a volley of questions at him.

He replied quietly, 'Sister, have your lunch first. The children are hungry. We will discuss things afterwards.'

Lunch over, Mother put my two sisters to sleep. All this while I was listening to the talk between the two in Kannada. Vyankanna said, 'Bhimanna is not in Poona. I could not talk with that woman for long. We'll wait till tomorrow.' Then he, too, stretched himself and went to sleep. Mother slept next to my sisters; she covered her face with her sari and began to weep quietly. I nestled close to her; we patted and tried to console each other. The first two days and nights were spent listening to the sound of engine whistles, but there was no sign of Bhimanna. Mother became desperate on the third day and insisted that my uncle go to Bhimanna again and find out the truth of the matter. As per the rules of the charity home, travellers were allowed to stay for only three days. Hence the impatience on Mother's part.

That afternoon Vyankanna brought Bhimanna with him and we began to dance with joy. He caressed us all and looked at Mother. 'God knows how long we are going to be left to the mercy of the winds,' Mother said while weeping bitterly.

Bhimanna said nothing but looked very serious. He asked uncle to get a horse carriage. After Vyankanna left, Bhimanna moved closer to Mother and put his hand on her back, but she pushed it away immediately.

We rode in the carriage to a tenement with a tiled roof. The board on the wall read 'Vaidikashram'. A dark man clad in white came forward, held Bhimanna's hand with a smile, and they spoke in Kannada. He was Mr Kulkarni, a professor in Deccan College. We were accommodated in one of his two rooms and thus began our stay in Vaidikashram. I was enrolled in Bhave Primary School.

Bhimanna picked me up on his bicycle and dropped me to school every day, singing along the way. Pedestrians would stop to look at him with curiosity; some of them knew him and nodded in appreciation. At all times I have seen Bhimanna like this, always deeply immersed in music.

After a couple of months, Bhimanna moved us to Jeevan Restaurant on Tilak Road, where we stayed for three months. Rekha and Chitra, sisters and Marathi film stars, were our neighbours. They asked Mother whether my younger sister could play a small role in a movie being filmed at that time. Mother declined.

'She' had strongly objected to our arrival in Poona. Therefore, we were being moved from one place to the other. All said and done, good upbringing and emotional involvement kept Bhimanna bound to us in these circumstances as well.

We next moved to two rooms in 'Swadhyay', a bungalow next to Deccan Gymkhana on Bhandarkar Road. Here began a new experiment—that of staying with 'her' under one roof. This turned out to be a painful trial for Mother as she was reduced to the position of a maidservant, who had to take care of all the household chores and listen to the taunts of 'her' sisters. In fact, if a visitor inquired about Mother, 'she' would say, 'She is the house maid'. 'She' was already pregnant when she came to Poona from Nagpur and 'her' child was born here. Mother had to look after 'her' child when 'she' retired for afternoon naps. She also had to accept 'her' intimacy with Bhimanna. What else could she do except weep with us in her lap?

Recently, I had an occasion to talk to the daughter-in-law of the owner of Swadhyay. She is quite old now, but she told me many stories about that period. She recalled how Mother would sometimes lose patience and shout in desperation to Bhimanna, 'Look after your children. I am going to kill myself', and then start running on the streets. 'My mother-in-law would then ask me to follow your mother, lest she really did something serious to herself, and left you children orphans.'

I recall yet another incident when we were living there and Vyankanna visited us. Bhimanna's guru, Sawai Gandharva, had settled in Poona and was not keeping well. He would secretly send some money to his guru after returning from a concert. 'She' objected to such 'squandering', but Bhimanna would not be cowed. One day he went out with Vyankanna in a great hurry. When he returned, he simply said, 'Guruji is no more ...' and left again.

I used to help Mother in her household chores. Once as I was crossing the threshold with a flour container in my hand, I slipped and hurt my forehead, the mark of which is still visible. 'She' once chastised me when I plucked a couple of guavas from the tree in the backyard of the house. Mother kept pestering Bhimanna for a separate accommodation for us 'at any cost'. She took my sisters to her elder sister Premakka in Belgaum for a few days, and I was sent to Bhimanna's new house 'Ambuniwas' near Badshah Restaurant on Tilak Road, close to my school.

'Her' mother lived in Awate Apartments near Perugate where I would go with Bhimanna every evening and come back late. I often looked after 'her' child, who used to sit in a basket in front of Bhimanna's bicycle. I would be half-dead with hunger and sleep, and sometimes missed a step or two. 'She' would shout at me, 'Are you blind or what?' On the way we would buy bread and I would eat it and go to bed. I was attending morning school. By the time school was over I would be starving again. I suffered in silence, and I would sleep flat on my empty stomach to suppress my hunger. Bhimanna would occasionally give me money to buy bananas, and this loving gesture was enough to satisfy me.

Finally we moved to an old room with a tin roof in the Limaye Wadi area of Sadashiv Peth, which 'she' had selected for us. Mother returned from Belgaum and settled down in this new place. We three children were admitted to schools. Bhimanna would visit us regularly, morning and evening. By now he had gained popularity and was in great demand.

I can never forget the kindness of our neighbours and friends who gave us so much love and care while in Nagpur. Even after we moved to Poona, affectionate people like Sitakant Lad, an officer at Nagpur radio station, made it a point to see us whenever he happened to be in town. He and his wife had been witness to our suffering and showered love on us all. They once had even purchased all the balloons from a vendor and gave them to us.

Once Bhimanna came and said to me, 'You have been asking for a bicycle. Go to the corner shop and get one from there.' I rushed out and brought back one of medium height that he had already selected for me. The owner of the shop, a wrestler, was a friend of Bhimanna's. However, after six months, only the chassis remained intact, in its original form, as all the other parts had to be replaced. Bhimanna was a trusting person and never bothered to check the genuineness of an object. Later on in my life I enjoyed using several other vehicles, but the happiness which that bicycle brought to me was unmatched: I would wander through the streets of the city like a bird that had got new wings.

The violin maestro Prabhakar Jog, also known as 'Tatya', was our neighbour. The immortal song sequence of Gajanan Madgulkar's *Geet Ramayan* was composed at his place. Singers and instrumentalists visited him for practice and I enjoyed listening to them. He was always well-dressed and was a cheerful person. I would wait at the gate of the building and run back shouting, 'Bhimanna *bandaru*' (Bhimanna has come). Tatya would mimic me and make everybody laugh. His elder sister, a widow, and her son Dhananjay lived with him. She was an affectionate lady and used to call me 'Gharuanna'. Anna Joshi, the tabla expert, befriended me for a special reason: whenever he came from Bombay, where he lived, he would need my bicycle, which I willingly lent him. In return, he would sometimes play his *dholki* only for me and I would be in seventh heaven listening to him.

We were shuttled from place to place, like the displaced after the Partition, but finally we settled in Sadashiv Peth. As in an overnight coup, we had become the behind-the-curtain people in Bhimanna's life. The moment he returned from a performance, 'she' would grab his earnings. It was 'she' who decided how much was to be doled out to us. Bhimanna was helpless, and it often led to altercations between them. After all, he did have a conscience!

Once when I happened to go to Bhimanna's house, Ambuniwas, I saw a police cordon there. The Minister for Information and Broadcasting B.V. Keskar was visiting him. By this time Bhimanna had earned a big name in government circles. The use of the harmonium, a musical instrument of accompaniment, had been banned on All India Radio. Bhimanna vehemently opposed the ban, which was eventually lifted. The harmonium is a very effective accompanying instrument as it gives a melodious support to the singing, but some bureaucrats, in their short-sightedness, had put a ban on it.

Subsequently, Indira Gandhi became the minister for Information and Broadcasting. She was Bhimanna's fan. Indeed, whoever came in contact with him became his friend and fan. And the ordinary audience simply idolized him. He developed a pattern for his concerts. He would start with a khayal (extended exposition of a raga), follow it with a thumri (a light composition), and then follow it by a natya sangeet (a stage song). Then, he would pause for an intermission, after which a badakhayal (a slow and steady beginning to express the mood of the raga) would be presented. The performance would finally be rounded off with a Bhairavi (a morning raga). It was a melodious journey. All types of people sat in the audience—commoners, scholars, connoisseurs. Time was never a constraint. He would pour his heart and soul into the performance. It was, indeed, his great luck that highly appreciative and willing listeners comprised the audience.

In those days Poona offered a continuing feast of intellectual and cultural food with various scholars, artists, and orators addressing people on different occasions and on different topics. It was, indeed, the cultural centre of India. Musical concerts took place frequently in the city. As I made the most of such opportunities, it worked in a significant way to shape and cultivate my tastes. I was never attracted to cheap joys and forms of entertainment as my tastes had been honed and refined in childhood.

The school, too, played a role in shaping my mind as the library was well stocked with good books. I developed a liking for reading which has continued till today. I began with books about Tarzan, about Sinbad the Sailor, and *Aesop's Fables*. There was a second-hand bookshop close to our house where one could sit for hours and read against a small payment. I would spend the whole day there during holidays. For a time I was fascinated by heroes like Chhotu, Kala Pahad, Jhunjhar— the protagonists of Baburao Arnalkar's detective stories. Once I brought home one such book and Bhimanna happened to see it. He, too, became a fan and, in a chance meeting with Lata Mangeshkar at an airport, he advised her to carry those books with her for fighting boredom on a flight.

Soon I became a voracious reader and devoured anything and everything that came within my reach, such as the complete works of Veer Savarkar, biographies of revolutionaries, fiction by great novelists like H.N. Apte, Sane Guruji, V.S. Khandekar, Acharya Atre, P.B. Bhave, S.N. Pendse, and N.S. Phadke, and also the mildly erotic books of Chandrakant Kakodkar.

Although we were living in only one room in Limaye Wadi, the yard was spacious and clean. There were two trees—one *champa* and the other *prajakt*—that would shed a shower of its fragrant flowers. I was cultivating a small flower garden in one corner and watered it regularly. Running water was available for the whole day and the yard could be kept clean. Open drains giving out a foul smell were unknown in Poona. Municipal tankers used to wash the roads in summers. Every Sunday I visited the central vegetable market to buy fresh vegetables, and I learnt the market ways. My school stood at a stone's throw from our house, and my friends and I spent hours on end tiring ourselves out with different games. I had a pet dog, Shyamya, for whom Bhimanna often brought bread and butter and with whom he would often play.

Nearby stood a small, clean Shiva temple surrounded by huge trees. Sitting in the shade of the temple I would often practise the notes that I had heard during Bhimanna's performances. I felt immense joy in doing that—I was like a new swimmer enjoying every dive into the water. It thrilled me, and I began to understand the nature of the various ragas in the light of what I had heard from Bhimanna. It was as if I had learnt the secret code to open Ali Baba's cave!

There were several other temples around us, among which the Narad temple was especially interesting; kirtan performances by good singers were a regular feature here. I used to listen to the Ramayana series with rapt attention. At one corner of the street was the temple of Pawan Maruti. Watching the diverse traffic from its stone platform was an exciting diversion. Near this temple was the Shivaji Mandir with a small courtyard where we played. Bhimanna had performed there once. Sometimes I used to attend the Sangha *Shakha* (daily activities held in the various branches of the Rashtriya Swayamsevak Sangh) held there and I enjoyed the sonorous notes of the Sanskrit prayer sung every day.

The practice of songs from *Geet Ramayan* used to be held in Prabhakar Jog's house, where I spent hours listening hungrily to the melodies. Great singers like Babuji (Sudhir Phadke) and others used to be present there. Master Krishnarao Phulambrikar lived in the vicinity and could be heard singing while one walked through the lanes and by-lanes. Indeed, these people lived in their own world of music.

My school, Bhave Primary School, boasted of a galaxy of talented teachers. While D.S. Desai spoke on the political happenings in the country, K.P. Joshi, S.A. Shukla, and C.R. Athalye were harsh disciplinarians. Mr Joshi taught English and was quick to slap us across our cheeks if we made grammatical mistakes. Mr Shukla taught us Marathi and always liked my essays. He even read them out to the class, silencing my rivals who called me '*yandu-gundu*', a common jibe at Kannada speakers. He helped develop a good literary taste in us. Our Hindi teacher C.B. Onkar always wore a rose in his buttonhole. To improve our vocabulary, he would give ten synonyms for one word in Hindi. His way of punishing was to tickle us madly.

On the eve of the annual social gathering, our teacher Mr Parchure would trace me out to present the opening

31

prayer '*Ishastavan*'. All the teachers were like coconuts—hard from outside, but tender and loving in their hearts. They would feed us well during excursions. Although we were economically stable now, our teacher Mr Athalye allowed me 50 per cent concession in the tuition fees after reading the entry 'singing' as the source of family income. Our science teacher Mr Bapat always dressed formally in a suit and tie, was a model for us all. Our drawing teachers Mr Phadke and Mr Bhide were the very models of kindness. They groomed me for tests in drawing and taught me the basics of drawing—nature, free hand, memory, and so on, which stood me in good stead in later life. These people laid the foundations of our lives.

I was a lanky youth then, just a bag of bones, but I was very agile. Vyankanna's advice was to 'start a diet of white potato [egg] with milk to fill you out'. I had it for a few days, but soon developed a dislike for it. During the long vacations a passion for physical workout would possess us. We would go to the gym and sweat it out there. One day we saw a man preparing bhang (a drink of cannabis leaves mixed with milk) there. We took to our heels and the gym visits stopped.

Mother was always particular about teaching us good manners and habits. If any of us left food half-eaten on our plates, she would shout at us, 'My husband burns a bowlful of his blood when he gives a concert. The money for this food comes from his blood. Take heed. Don't ever waste food!' She would never tire of reminding us, 'You are the sons of the Joshi family. Use your brains, work hard, and eat well. Eating food without earning, it is charity and alms from the graveyard. The Joshis don't live like parasites.' 'Earn your food and honour, don't aspire to being affluent parasites.' That was what she kept reminding us.

Once the Sawai Gandharva Sangeet Mahotsav was held in our school complex. For the first time in my life I listened to a full-fledged concert by great performers. The sitar maestro Ustad Vilayat Khan gave the performance of his life that night. He made his silver-studded instrument sing! The notes haunted me the next day when I was writing my math examination at school. As a result, I could answer only half of the questions.

Mr Parchure would sometimes make me sit up on the table in the classroom and say, 'You are the son of a singer, sing us a song'. I would sing one of Bhimanna's compositions, imitating his gesticulations. I was a good performer, as some of my contemporaries recalled later.

Bhimanna tried to strike a balance between his two households. Whenever he returned from a performance, he would bring spices and clothes for us. Once he brought me sharkskin trousers and nylon manilas and dresses for my sisters from Calcutta. We wore them with pride as none of our friends had such fine outfits. He brought rasgullas too. He was very pleased about his success and popularity and once when he visited us before leaving for a concert, he kissed all of us, including our mother, right under our noses! We were stunned. When he bought a used Fox motorbike, he gave me a long ride through the city. He took the whole family for a ride when he purchased his Dodge car. 'Quick! Hurry up!' he said and took us all to a restaurant in the cantonment area where we ate good food to our hearts' content. Overall he was an affectionate soul.

Mother had noted my interest in and talent for singing, and she enrolled me in the Marathe Class of Music at a social club. I soon got tired of the teaching as it did not capture my heart. I missed 'Bhimsen' in the lessons. Mother was quite particular about our performance in school; she was worried lest my love of music take me along my father's path, so she stopped my tuitions. Even so, my passion for music did not lessen. I continued to learn from Bhimanna himself while listening to his performances whenever an opportunity presented itself. I would sometimes hold an empty bucket before my mouth to get the effects of the lower notes. I am told that a similar monitoring technique is used in modern times, too, for listening one's own notes. Bhimanna himself often used to cover one ear with his palm to check the exact quality of a note.

On the 'other' side of the house, the young heir apparent was being trained by the noted vocalist Pandit Chandrakant Kapileshwari. Such luxury was not for us. One would like to think that Bhimanna wished to avoid for us the uncertainties and insecurities that a professional performer faces because he paid greater attention to my performance at school rather than my music lessons.

My thread ceremony was planned when I turned ten. I was given a silk suit and a gold locket. The ceremony was to be held at Premakka's house, my maternal aunt in Belgaum, for the convenience of my grandparents and other relatives. Mother took Sumangala with her and went in advance for the ceremony. Bhimanna, Usha, and I joined them later. We all travelled first class. For years to come, I remembered the good breakfast with toast and jam and tea served in a pot. Those were the happy days of life when good moments came our way.

The thread ceremony took place with great fanfare in a pandal specially erected in front of Tatacharya Pangari's house in Tilak Wadi. A ceremonial procession was taken out. Six months earlier, when Damodar uncle's thread ceremony had taken place, Mother had asked my grandfather about mine. He had responded with silence. When my ceremony took place with such lavish arrangements, he said to Bhimanna, 'If that was how you wanted it, I, too, could have done it here in Gadag.' Bhimanna gave no answer although his look said clearly that he, too, was quite capable of doing things on a grand scale on his own.

A party was arranged in Poona as well to which 'she' was invited. Someone asked me to sing a song that Bhimanna liked. So I sang a composition in raga Jogiya, *'Hari ka bhed na payo'* (Never understood the difference between Rama and Hari). People liked it, but 'her' face showed disapproval. 'She' could not bear my showing musical talent at such a young age.

It was my duty to go to Ambuniwas to fetch money from Bhimanna for running the household. A staircase led to a passage, with the kitchen in front and a spacious drawing room on the right. Bhimanna used to sleep there, on his stomach, wearing a sleeveless vest and striped pyjamas. Late-night programmes required him to sleep long hours, unless he had to give another concert immediately. He was well built and I liked his looks. He had curly hair and his body smelt of tulsi oil. I would sit there massaging his feet gently and softly calling out his name a couple of times. He would ask, 'Is it Raghu? Wait a minute.' Meanwhile, I would look at the portraits of Sawai Gandharva and Rahimat Khan with his flowing beard. There was also a lifelike portrait of Lokmanya Tilak on the wall. A shelf held some books on Hindustani classical music. I once saw Bhimanna taking down notes about a raga from a book written by Pandit Bhatkhande. He would get up leisurely, yawn loudly, and give me a smile. I was always reluctant to make him get up, but I had no choice. If he went on a week-long tour, then the money was late in coming, but the payments refused to wait.

After waking up, he would have a wash and go to 'her' to ask for money. The demand was invariably met with reluctance. Occasionally Bhimanna had to raise his voice. Then 'she' would ask him, 'Are you going to squander all your money on strangers?' I used to be stunned to hear the word 'strangers'. How were we strangers? I could never make out. If Bhimanna were on a tour and had left money for us with 'her', 'she' would not give the entire amount at one time. 'She' would make me run to and fro several times. Once 'she' even insisted that the money had been given to me and 'she' did not know what had happened to it. One day when I went to that house, 'she' was putting butter on bread. The moment 'she' saw me, 'she' hid it.

'She' would pester Bhimanna to train 'her' whenever Sawai Gandharva Sangeet Mahotsav was round the corner. During the training sessions, I would sit on the staircase and learn what Bhimanna was teaching 'her'. He would make 'her' learn by rote, usually raga *Puriya Kalyan* or *Puriya Dhanashree*. Bhimanna would lose patience with 'her'. On the stage, too, 'her' performance, even for a short duration, was a struggle. Often the audiences booed 'her' out. I was witness to 'her' discomfiture. In an interview Bhimanna once referred to 'her' as his guru, which was clearly said ironically. I was furious when I heard it said that it was 'she' who had taught Bhimanna some specific ragas!

Bhimanna was in charge of purchasing groceries when Mother needed these. He would ride on his bicycle and buy these in bigger quantities than what Mother had asked for. He had, as it were, signed the 'giving pledge' in life. The same style ruled his performances too. Once when the kerosene stove was not working, Bhimanna instantly took it and returned with a new one. The shopkeeper had obviously managed to convince him that the old stove was beyond repair. Probably a pinch of tobacco had done the trick! But the new stove would not work either. How could it? After all, it needed to be filled with oil which Bhimanna had forgotten to decant from the old stove! Again Bhimanna went off on his bicycle with a raga on his lips. How could Mother let go such a good chance to make a good jibe? I heard her describing to a neighbour how this man was a total dunderhead in the practical world!

During the long school vacations, we would go to Premakka in Belgaum. Bhimanna knew that we would not be able to stand the cold, so he sent half a dozen woollen rugs for us with Appa Jalgaonkar, his harmonium accompanist. Sometimes Premakka would visit us with her children. She was affectionate and an unfailing support for Mother. I was her favourite and would be given two cups of tea to beat Belgaum's bitter winter. I can still visualize Tilak Wadi where I would sit, eating her *poha* (shallow-fried rice flakes with spices) served with raw onion, perched on a champa tree. Bhimanna once bought a camera and took a few photographs of Mother, which pleased her immensely. Such moments were few and far between; most times, there were altercations and arguments.

On the auspicious occasion of Lakshmi puja during Diwali, Mother would send me to Bhimanna to fetch a new currency note as good omen. There, too, preparations for the festival would be in progress. The sight of me would turn 'her' away while Bhimanna would ask what had brought me there. On giving him Mother's message, he would go inside and ask 'her' for a new, crisp currency note. 'She' would grumble and object, and Bhimanna, too, seemed unwilling. This hurt me as I could see a fat wad of notes in a tray ready for their puja.

I was the proverbial ping-pong ball between 'her', Bhimanna, and Mother. What a contrast between the two scenarios! That is how I felt on such occasions. Those who have had a comfortable childhood can hardly know how excruciating the entire time was for us. One cannot overcome one's bitterness against such treatment. I used to be angry with Bhimanna, too, which was the natural reaction of a young son.

Once on the occasion of Holi Mother made the customary *puran poli*s (wheat chapatti with sweet stuffing of gram paste). She gave me some prasad (sacred food offering) on a banana leaf to be fed to a cow. I set out for the Shiva temple looking for a cow when I saw Bhimanna approaching. 'Looks like lunch is ready,' he said. 'Yes, I am taking this for the cow,' I replied. When I returned home, the banana-leaf plates had been laid out, and Bhimanna and my sisters had sat down to eat. He had half a dozen hot puran polis doused in pure ghee. Then he stopped and said, 'I must get up from the meal a little hungry. I have to eat *there* too.' That day Mother's happiness knew no bounds. She had been brought up in a culture where a wife's duty was to provide bountifully to her husband whatever he wanted and whenever he demanded, whereas some people were trained to recover the price for every pleasure they gave.

On the occasion of Rath Saptami puja, Mother always asked me to buy small earthen pots which she filled with milk and placed on fire till the milk spilt over into the fire. This was a customary ritual, an offering to the Sun God. 'On this day your father was born, brilliant like the sun. Pray for his good health and glory,' she told us. We would all pray to the sun with folded hands and touch Bhimanna's feet with our heads.

We had some good neighbours. A highly cultured family, the Gores, lived in the same block. They greatly respected

Bhimanna, and Nalini Aunty showered love and care on me as they had no children. I got many books from them. I continued to visit them even after we moved to a different house.

I can never forget two old ladies living below the staircase. One of them, Durgatai, had a son posted as a collector somewhere. Once he came with a box of sweets to see her. His wife, however, did not step out of her car parked outside on the road. Durgatai lived an extremely austere life in that small room, slept on a thin carpet, and earned her living by making incense sticks. Mother would often send food to her, and she, too, occasionally called us for lunch, which we enjoyed despite being cramped up in that small space. On such occasions she would secretly wipe away her tears, thinking of her son and grandchildren whom she seldom saw.

Another lady, Chandorkar Aji, was fair, fat, and lived by herself. She had a little bigger space under another staircase and earned her livelihood as a cook. She would sometimes cook for us, and her *batata wada*s (spiced, deep-fried boiled potato mash with onion and garlic, coated with gram paste) were simply incomparable in taste. 'Growing children need good food,' she would tell Mother. She continued to visit us even after we moved elsewhere. Both the old women lived out their lonely days under the staircase of the building. These women and Mother had something common in their lives, which brought them close to each other.

Our neighbours Vaidya, the bicycle dealer, and Abhyankar were dedicated volunteers at the three-day Sawai Gandharva Sangeet Mahotsav every year. They were great fans of Bhimanna. He was very fond of the paan prepared by Abhyankar who supplied him regularly with these. I was always kept informed about Bhimanna's concerts so that I could attend these.

Generally I kept a very low profile as I was a shy boy. Our circumstances had made me so. But, of course, after the concerts were over, I would touch Bhimanna's feet before leaving. He would speak a sentence or two only if 'she' was not around.

Having kept company with such lovers of music, I got to know several interesting stories about artists. Bhimanna gave his best performance if the audience included well-informed and dignified persons. Some of them were Sardar Abasaheb Mujumdar, Mr Atre (music maestro Dr Prabha Atre's father), Dr Nanasaheb Deshpande (the son-in-law of Sawai Gandharva), maestro Vasantrao Deshpande, and Dattopant Deshpande. They were all fine connoisseurs of classical music. I used to read from their faces whether the performance was up to the mark or not. At about the same time, the Government of India invited Bhimanna to participate in the cultural troupe which was to visit Afghanistan. Members of the royal family there had heard Bhimanna's recorded performances and hence he was a special invitee. He excelled there as well. When he visited us before leaving for the tour, dressed in a woollen suit, he looked smart.

One fine morning Bhimanna came with a man carrying a big box. It contained a radio set for us. It was a big, twelve-band set. The aerial was put up and the music started to play. The first song that we heard, and greeted with thunderous claps, was the popular number *'Hasale mani chandane'* (The moon smiles in my mind), sung by the veteran singer Manik Varma. Bhimanna watched Mother's response as he enjoyed his tea. After he left, the neighbours thronged and we had a feast of songs over tea because, at that time, a radio was still a rarity. We used to flock around it whenever the national programme of music featured Bhimanna's performance, and would be thrilled at the announcement of his name in English and in Hindi. These moments were matchless when I would be filled with pride as Bhimanna opened with his sonorous lower notes and the rich sounds of the tanpura filled the air with sweetness. These were the unforgettable moments of joy in my life.

Three

I THINK THIS HAPPENED in Badami. I woke up to the mel-
lifluous notes of Bhimanna who was starting on his usual
morning *riyaz* (practice). I snuggled closer, rested my head on
his lap, and drank those unearthly notes thirstily. He smiled
at me, cleared his throat once, spat in the spittoon, and
resumed the riyaz. I was barely five or six then, but the memory of that experience refuses to go away and it continues to
thrill me even today. Dressed in immaculate white, he paused
for a minute, picked me up, and kissed me on my cheek. The
fragrance of his body and the touch of his hairy chest come back
to me even now, as if I had experienced them just a minute
ago. It was always the same during his riyaz, and surely it
planted the seed of love and admiration for him in my heart.
I began to look upon my father as a man with a body of iron
resonating with music. His riyaz would last eight hours at a
stretch, and my listening time synchronized with it, impart-
ing a basic firmness to the notes emanating from my own
throat, though I am not well versed in the grammar of each
and every raga. Whether a tanpura accompanies my singing
or not, whenever I close my eyes those notes start resonating
in my mind and I start walking on the path shown by my
'musical' father.

I grew up with different stories about Bhimanna as told
to me by various elders, aunts, uncles, and my grandfather.

To every one of them, he was their 'Bhimu'. They made me aware that my father was a genius. I kept making a clear mental recording of whatever they told me.

Childhood proclaims the man in the making: Bhimanna proclaimed the vocal maestro in him right from his childhood. At the age of three, he taught his mother how to sing Purandara Dasa's bhajan '*Aadisidalu Yashode*' (Yashoda played with Krishna). With his black mane and shining eyes, he was already the apple of everyone's eye, the firstborn son of the Joshi clan. His father, Guracharya, was an eminent scholar of the classics as well as of English. Deeply religious, he spent hours in pujas and other rituals every day. The house would be redolent with the fragrance of lamps burning with pure ghee, camphor, and tulsi. Added to it were the mantras sung by him sonorously in chaste Sanskrit, which Bhimu listened with rapt attention. He taught Bhimu the entire Sanskrit thesaurus of *Amarakosha*, which Bhimu, with his razor-sharp intellect, internalized faultlessly. This was the food which Bhimu was fed in childhood. Years of this learning emerged in his rendering of *santwani* (the words of the saints).

Added to his brilliance and comprehension was his passion for music. As a child, if he heard music from a procession going down the road, he would rush out, even if naked, and join the singers and musicians. He would return home only after they had ceased their singing and playing. He would hide himself in a circus tent for days only to listen to the band playing there. As a last resort, my grandfather stuck the home address on Bhimu's shirt so that wherever he was found he could be sent back home!

Bhimu lived in a rented house with his parents. One night, when he was three, his father was awakened by the sound of a heavy thud downstairs. Bhimu was not to be seen anywhere.

When he came down, he saw Bhimu drinking water from a big jar. When his father tried to help him, Bhimu waved him away, finished drinking, and went back to his bed. It was not in his nature to depend on others for any help.

Bhimu was fond of animals. He brought home eight puppies and hid them in a corner. As bread and milk began to disappear in great quantities, his mother did a bit of investigation and solved the mystery: the puppies were sent back. Once while chasing a chicken he entered the henhouse and, surrounded by all hens, could not get out. To comfort himself he started singing a bhajan that his mother used to sing.

Bandekaka, Bhimanna's uncle, once told me that Bhimu rode his father's bicycle when he was six. His street acrobatics include a threesome on the bicycle with a string of scorpions tied to the handle! He was good at all games, especially football. He was an expert swimmer trained by his father, and also a supple *mallakhamb* (vertical pole) player. During school inspection, the inspector would make a special request for Bhimu's mallakhamb demonstration. Both father and son, then, would hold the spectators spellbound for an hour. He was a strong, young boy and had a wide circle of friends. There used to be frequent complaints against him. Once he kicked the ball so hard that he hit a player, who fell down and lay senseless for a whole day; that put a stop to his playing football. Whenever I heard of those feats, I felt proud and began to believe that Bhimanna was a superman.

Bhimu and his younger brother Narayan were asleep on the terrace one day when a serpent started crawling over them. Aware of the danger, Bhimu softly told his brother to not make any movement. 'It will go away, it won't harm us,' he whispered. And that was what happened. The word 'fear' did not feature in his dictionary.

Once he had gone to Badami on the occasion of the Chaitra Padwa festival. A large monkey ran away with the silver glass kept on top of the *gudhi* (the ceremonial flag). No one was brave enough to chase the monkey and get it back. It was a challenge, and Bhimanna accepted it. He jumped onto the terrace and the race began. Both were exhausted after two hours of running, but finally Bhimanna caught hold of the animal and dealt it with a couple of hard blows. The monkey gave in, released the silver glass, and escaped. Bhimu liked to accept challenges and his only aim was to win. And that is how he performed later on in his concerts.

When grandfather Guracharya was living in a small town, cooking was done on fire using wood brought by woodcutters. Once the wood was wet and had to be kept outside the house. The next morning it had disappeared as the town bully had stolen it. When Guracharya went to him with a request to return it, the thief retorted, 'Is your name written on it?' Grandfather said nothing and went to school. The next day Bhimanna heard from his mother what had happened. He asked his father to keep his bicycle outside the house early next morning. When Guracharya woke up, he saw that Bhimanna had brought back on his bicycle all the firewood and kept it properly heaped up. Shortly, the bully turned up and asked about the firewood. Bhimanna shouted at the top of his voice, 'Is your ***'s name written on it?' Bhimanna made such a scene that people from the whole lane gathered around. The bully realized that he had taken on someone who was bolder than him, and took to his heels. Vyankanna told me that for this service Bhimanna extracted two laddus smeared with ghee from his mother!

By now Bhimanna's love for music was well-entrenched in him. Narayankaka told us that when he was playing the role of Lord Krishna at a school performance, he chanted Krishna's well-known verses so effectively that the audience felt as if they were listening to the Lord himself:

Arjuna, whenever faith falters
And evil tendencies rise, then I take birth
To protect the good and destroy the evil ones;
I take birth again and again to protect faith....

He also played the role of Mahatma Gandhi's wife Kasturba, with his head covered and working at the spinning wheel, and no one could make out who the actor was.

Bhimanna was the favourite of my maternal grandfather, who was also his maternal uncle. Grandfather Guracharya did not like his son being pampered by his rich maternal uncle. While his father performed the routine morning puja, Bhimanna would get ready for school after breakfast. But everything depended on his mood: for him skipping school was not unusual. He would be listening to the vocal maestro Abdul Karim Khan Sahib's records in a restaurant and, returning home late at night, he would sneak through the bathroom window, enter the kitchen, eat the dinner kept covered by his mother, and go to bed. Although his father had instructed her never to keep food for him, his mother could not bear to think of her son going hungry.

A childhood friend of Bhimanna once told me during my Gadag stay that Guracharya wanted to groom Bhimanna as a classical scholar like him, but Bhimanna had other inclinations. He would climb up to the dome of the town temple, sing as long as he wished, swim in a well as much as he wanted to with his friends, and work out vigorously in the akhara. Once when he dived into a well, he hit a boulder at the bottom and broke an incisor, which could be seen whenever he opened his mouth to sing. Later, he had a gold tooth put in its place.

Every year he participated in the power games competition. Bhimanna and his friend could bend an iron bar and break small iron nails with just two fingers. They used to be taken in a procession to Lakshmi Theatre where they were publicly felicitated. Bhimanna was always the best in every activity, but what he ultimately chose to do was the right decision. Indeed, he was a stormy young man in his young days!

Things came to a head once when his father read Bhimanna's school report card: failed in all subjects! As a matter of fact he had remained absent from the examination. 'Bring him to me when he comes home or else I will thrash you all,' declared Guracharya. When he came home, the siblings pounced on him and took him to their father, who ordered a cane to be brought. Someone brought a small cane with which he started whipping; but then he asked for a longer, stronger one, with which he showered blows ceaselessly on Bhimanna's back. Bhimanna stood unmoved, his hands folded on his chest. When his mother tried to intervene, his father pushed her away violently and the caning continued. The whole family was terror-struck and dumb with fear. Finally Guracharya was exhausted and asked Bhimanna, 'What, after all, are you going to do in life?' Bhimanna coolly declared, 'I am only going to sing.'

Guracharya threw away the cane and went into his room. Repentant and relenting, he rubbed oil and turmeric on Bhimanna's bleeding body. Narayankaka told me that after that incident Guracharya never raised a finger to punish Bhimanna. Indeed, he was not cut out for ordinary things.

Ramabai, Bhimanna's mother, often scolded him over his madness for music. 'Are you ever going to work for a living?'

she would ask him. When he got tired of hearing this, he said, 'The day will come when I will shower money on you!' Alas! She did not live to see the crown of glory and prestige placed on Bhimanna's head, and died soon after his marriage.

Eventually, in 1933, at the age of eleven, Bhimanna ran away from home in search of a guru. When the attic of the house was being cleaned, a few dried-up laddus were found lying there. Bhimanna had flung them in a rage as he would never accept only one a time; he always wanted two. His father's eyes welled up on seeing the dried-up sweets as he recalled his son's memories.

Hema Aunty recalls that when Bhimanna ran away from home to learn music, his mother was traumatized and stopped eating properly. She only had a single meal in a day. Tears flowed almost non-stop from her eyes. When he returned finally after three years, he had developed a strong physical body with the rich food and milk of Punjab where he had gone, and was sporting a beard. Vyankanna, Bhimanna's brother, recalls that his mother recognized him only from his eyes and the two wept bitterly in each other's embrace for a long time. Then he went to Kundgol to learn singing from Sawai Gandharva, who agreed to be his guru. Bhimanna stayed at his house in the *guru–shishya* (teacher–disciple) tradition. He slogged there ceaselessly and had to do every kind of work as part of the guru's fees.

Guracharya and his brother Ramacharya paid a visit to Kundgol to see how Bhimanna was progressing. After the customary glass of water had been offered to the visitors, his father asked, 'How is Bhimu doing?' but the guru didn't answer. There was no sight of Bhimu for a long time, until finally they saw him carrying two huge pitchers full of water. As he started to pour it into the tank in front of the house, he fainted. His father helped him to sit down. Bhimu was running a temperature. His father was about to address the guru angrily when the guru said indifferently, 'You may take your son away this minute'. When Bhimu heard this he told his father, 'I'm all right here. You may leave now.' Both guru and student matched each other in their unyielding spirit.

Sawai Gandharva often sent Bhimanna to Hubli for various tasks. Gurubhagini Gangubai Hangal also lived in Hubli. Bhimanna would unfailingly visit her, enjoy his favourite poha, and talk about music. When the guru learnt about this he was angry. The next time Bhimanna was with Gangubai, he saw his guru walking towards the house. Gangubai hid Bhimanna in the bathroom. The teacher was in a huff and asked if Bhimanna had come to visit her, which Gangubai denied. The guru stayed on and showed no sign of moving out. When he finally left, Bhimanna, half-choked by the smouldering firewood in the bathroom, rushed out, sweating all over. 'A few minutes more and I would have surely suffocated there,' Bhimanna told Mother years later.

He also told Mother how the teaching began. One day while the training was in progress, some noise outside distracted Bhimanna. The guru threw a nutcracker at him, which hit him on the forehead and inflicted a deep wound. Bhimanna held his bleeding wound with one hand and the tanpura in the other, and the training continued. The guru's wife rushed out and stopped the lesson to tend to Bhimanna's wound. He bore this mark all his life. Whenever I gave him a massage, I would caress the scar and try to imagine the entire sequence of events as it happened. It was as if the guru had bestowed a blessing on his talented student to ward off all evil from his life!

The water-storing exercise in his youth damaged Bhimanna's muscles so badly that he suffered from pain in his shoulders throughout his life. Many taunted him then that he would die of water-storing. However, he proved that he was made of sterner stuff, and this eventually made him an all-time hero in his field.

Bhimanna was a deeply devout person and revered his father, mother, his own guru, and the family guru, Raghavendra Swami. The swami was a devotee of Rama and a follower of the Dvaita School of Philosophy and was regarded as an avatar of Prahlad, the great mythical devotee of Vishnu. He was a sanyasi, a celibate, and entered the yogic state of samadhi at Vrindavan. A large number of devotees had experienced the fruits of his grace.

Guracharya told me one of his own personal spiritual experiences. He had to go to Bangalore for some assessment work at an examination. There was a shortcut to the railway station from his house. He was in the habit of going to the station much in advance. As he was going out through the gate, he felt that someone was trying to pull him back. So he waited for a while and started again. He felt the pull again. He was convinced that it was some mysterious warning that he should cancel his Bangalore visit that day. The next day he read in the newspaper that the train on which he was to travel had met with a serious accident resulting in many casualties. He was convinced that the swami had saved him.

Bhimanna, too, was a great devotee of the swami and invariably visited his *math* (ashram) before his concerts. His own car once met with an accident on the Satara Road and almost slid down a hillside. 'Don't panic. Nothing bad will happen,' he shouted. The car slowly landed on a flat piece of land just below the slope, with minor scraping. All of them returned safely to Poona by another vehicle. 'The swami saved us,' he told Mother. 'Since death is inevitable, let me take the responsibility for my own death,' he said, and dismissed his driver. Thereafter, he drove himself everywhere, no matter how long the distance.

He was painfully aware that his second alliance had landed him in untold miseries, including the humiliations that our family had to put up with. One day he took out his car and drove towards Gadag in a rage. It was like a lion trying desperately to break open his cage and to set himself free. He reached Gadag late at night and found that his father had gone to a place in Koppal to chant a kirtan. He set out for Koppal, and found his father sleeping in the veranda of the math. He touched his feet and began to weep sorely. 'Tell me how to come out of this trap?' he asked. His father patted him on the head and replied, 'This is your doing and now you have to face it bravely'. Bhimanna stood up and set out on his return journey that very moment.

Damodar Uncle narrated this incident to me later. I often wondered why his father had said what he did. What had he meant by it? Had he been trying to disown his own responsibility as an elder? Only in my mature and calm moments did I understand what he had wanted to convey: we have to tend to our own sheep. We are responsible for our own doings and must never blame others for our sufferings. My grandfather remained detached in the same way all his life. He carried out his responsibility by educating the children he had from both his wives and then left them to their own devices.

Bhimanna's brother, Narayan, funded his own education and graduated as a metallurgist from Banaras Hindu University. Vyankatesh did his MSc, Madhav did his BCom, Madhu joined the navy and eventually qualified as a pilot in the Indian Air Force. Bhimanna took care of the expenses for Madhav's hospitalization during his illness. Both Madhav and Madhu led short lives. Among his sisters, Vanamala had a short life, but Hema lived on in Hebballi near Dharwad and died in February 2013.

Of Bhimanna's stepbrothers, Damodar became a bank employee after his matriculation. Vishal borrowed 5 rupees from his father to go to Bangalore, worked hard in many factories, and eventually rose to become the general manager of a packing factory and went to Qatar. Jayateerth became a cultural officer in the Karnataka government. He, too, had a short life. Sushilendra, Pranesh, and Vadiraj became traders. One of the brothers, Prakash, chose to become an agriculturist. Vishal helped his son to become an engineer.

Of his stepsisters, Parimala died, while Jyoti still lives in Hyderabad.

Four

AS THE ADAGE GOES, time and tide wait for none. Time passed on.

It was a cold Saturday morning and I lay snug in my bed. The gentle aroma of the boiling tea leaves caressed my nose. As soon as Mother poured the boiling concoction into a cup, I jumped out of bed and, after a speedy rinsing of the mouth, settled down close to the stove, holding the hot tea to stave off Poona's biting cold. Sipping tea sitting close to the warmth of the stove was one of my small pleasures.

Mother would often croon some bhajan of Purandara Dasa while she went about the household chores. One of my favourite bhajans describes how Hanuman's mother coaxes him, 'Get up, my precious one. It is time to be in the service of Rama. Sita is to be released and brought back. The treacherous Ravan is to be killed. There so much work to be done, get up quickly.' Mother sang very well. Her voice touched my heart. Bhimanna had taught her a few ragas before I was born. The courtyard would be redolent with the smell of flowers like the fragrant prajakt and the golden champa. My duty was to heat the bathwater. By the time my two sisters awoke, I was already on my way to school, which was a mere jump beyond the tin compound wall.

On that Saturday morning as I was preparing to leave for school, Bhimanna came to visit us. He was in a mood for bantering. 'What says the scorpion of Badami?' That was how he sometimes greeted Mother. (Badami was infested with red scorpions.) If I were awake, he would ask, 'How about your studies? Who are your teachers?' He would enjoy drinking tea while he practised the *taan* (singing swaras in a raga, in one interval between two matras, in fast tempo) and the *palte* (the raga swaras are taken in ascending and descending order while practising the raga) of a raga. The enticing smell of Mother's hot bhakris filled the room. Whenever Bhimanna was touring, he would invariably take with him these bhakris with groundnut chutney, *wangyachi bhaji* (brinjal mash bathed in oil), and curd-rice. He would stop in the middle of a taan and say, 'Let me taste the chutney with bhakri'. He would eat it holding it in his hand. Mother, too, would top the bhakri with a generous dollop of butter. 'Impatient, *always*!' A conspiratorial smile would flicker across their faces, which I could hardly understand then.

Bhimanna was an expert at mimicry. One Sunday when Mother had given us a vigorous oil massage and we were basking in the morning sunlight before our baths, Bhimanna entered and straightaway asked Mother, 'So, which movie was it yesterday?' We were surprised to hear that Mother had gone to see Bhagwan's popular movie *Albela* with her friends. Bhimanna had seen them near the theatre. 'Oh, I see!' he said when Mother told him the name of the movie. 'I will show you how Bhagwan dances.' And he performed a little jig, in perfect imitation of Bhagwan, to the popular number '*Sham dhale, khidki tale, tum seeti bajana chhod do*' (Stop whistling at my window in the evening)! We simply tumbled over each other laughing and the women hid their faces behind their sari pallus.

Bhimanna often lingered at our place till late in the night, but he would always return to the other house to sleep.

Once we children woke to loud altercations between him and Mother. She wanted him to stay over for the night but he insisted on leaving. When he refused, she shouted, 'I'm not a runaway wife. Our marriage has been solemnized in the presence of the gods and Brahmins.' She even tried to hold him back by his silk shirt, but he pulled it so violently that it tore and he left. Now she, too, felt challenged and said, 'All right! I too am leaving. Mind your children now.' She actually started running away and we followed her in consternation. She turned the corner near Pawan Maruti temple, leaving us all alone. We three froze in fear, crying bitterly, not knowing what to do. Someone took us to the Perugate police station.

Eventually, Mother's friend Kamal Kulkarni and her husband took charge of us and brought us home. Mother, who had gone to a relative's place, returned tearful. Only then were we reunited. We learnt later that all this time Bhimanna was hiding in 'her' mother's house right across the police station. The episode caused a lot of disturbance in Karnataka and the news reached my grandparents' house, but they said nothing. On the contrary they complained that Nandi (my mother) had torn off Bhimu's silk shirt! While my mother's married life was being torn to shreds, his parents chose to remain tongue-tied.

Mother was deeply hurt that all the seniors maintained a studied silence and turned their backs on their moral responsibilities. She often cursed them for her plight. But they were all basking in Bhimanna's glory. Besides, they knew that he was hard-headed and unlikely to change his mind. Why waste words! Though this was understandable to some extent, these elders could have at least cared for us, helped us, given us some love and affection, sheltered us sometimes in their homes. Life would have been at least a little more bearable for us. They were orthodox and followed all rituals religiously, but missed out on giving love to the world. Even the children from Bhimanna's generation got the same raw deal. We were their grandchildren, after all, if not their children! Bhimanna himself had opened his aching heart to me many a time saying that after his mother's demise, there was nothing left for him at his father's house.

By now Narayankaka had received his degree and was livid with anger when he learnt about Bhimanna's indiscretion. He confronted 'those' people and came to the conclusion that they were unrepentant and incorrigible. They deserved shooting in the arse! I often heard him say this. He wanted a redress for the unfair treatment given to us by his own brother. He even lodged a grievance with the then chief minister, Morarji Desai, and the wheels of inquiry began to move. One day Dr Nanasaheb Deshpande (Sawai Gandharva's son-in-law) came to us along with Bhimanna who promised volubly to redress the wrong and behave properly. Mother was asked to sign some papers, and the entire episode was patched up. But Bhimanna continued to nurse a grudge against his brother. The winds of 'women's liberation' had not yet started to blow, and Mother had no alternative but to put up with life's ill treatment, and to look after three children all by herself. Compared to the great sitar maestro Annapurna Devi, who also had to suffer neglect and ill treatment at the hands of her husband, the world-renowned sitar maestro Pandit Ravi Shankar, my mother was just a simple soul.

At about the same time, Narayankaka and Vyankanna had gone to Kundgol to invite Bhimanna's guru Sawai Gandharva to my aunt Hema's wedding. Sawai Gandharva was impressed by my uncles' qualifications and said, 'Joshi Master is lucky to have one son as an engineer and the other with an MSc degree and a job in hand. Excellent! But why are the elders in the family such crackpots? Why doesn't anyone sternly advise Bhimsen to look after his own wife and children, and not go philandering?'

Bhimanna sent us to Lakshmeshwara to attend Hema Aunty's wedding. 'She' took great care to keep him away from us. Bhimanna was not allowed to move about alone. The next day, after the wedding rituals were over, all of us went for a swim to the well. I didn't know how to swim, yet one of my uncles pushed me into the well. Thankfully, I was caught by another uncle and my grandfather, who were already in the water. I felt very comforted and consoled and was never scared of water again. In fact, I became an excellent swimmer. Guracharya himself was a good swimmer. Once he had jumped into a whirlpool to rescue Narayankaka. He brought two baskets full of sweet mangos, which we enjoyed over jokes and good conversation. He was fond of treating others with lavish foods.

The 'young prince', the firstborn of the other family, was a pampered child. His used pram was passed on to me as a gift which I loved a lot; I drove around my younger sister in it. One could see imported toys, too, in the other house. If I asked for a new notebook, I was lovingly advised by 'her' to use the blank pages in used notebooks. Bhimanna once refused to take me to Bombay, where he was performing, although I threw tantrums. I felt like puncturing his car's tyres. Finally he agreed and we went to Bombay in his Pontiac. I treasured my first vision of the city in my mind for a long time.

We left Poona for Bombay in the afternoon. Bhimanna picked me up from Limaye Wadi on the way. Bhimanna's accompanists, too, were travelling with us. We reached a sethji's bungalow at Chowpatty in the evening. Bhimanna was to perform at a private concert in a hall near the bungalow as the programme was sponsored by the sethji himself. Bhimanna concluded by 1:30 a.m. and we proceeded to Shivaji Park in Dadar. While he drove the car was filled with the fragrance of the mogra garlands that were hung in it. The next halt was at Suresh Haldankar's music school where Bhimanna was to give another performance. He regaled the audience with the soft notes of raga Lalit. The notes which he explored that day for over two hours vibrate in my memory even today and make my hair stand on end. I have come to believe that God himself had blessed Bhimanna with the choicest of ragas that he cultivated further through untiring efforts in riyaz.

The concert over, we returned to the same bungalow at Chowpatty. It was Bhimanna's habit to eat only after the performance was over and we all ate to our fill. We lay down to sleep and were still in deep slumber when, having put a paan daintily into his mouth, he called out loudly, 'Wake up! Come, let's enjoy the sunrise at Chowpatty.' It was early morning and we ambled to the beach with Bhimanna striding ahead. The surging waves inspired him to sing raga Todi. We woke up and listened with rapt attention. The harmonium maestro Thakurdas held my hand tightly and whispered in my ears, 'Raghu, listen carefully. You will never get to hear anything like this later.' It was as if Bhimanna's sonorous notes were in perfect tune with the sounds of the surging sea waves. All these years I have treasured those rare notes of *'Change nayanwa'* (Your eyes are beautiful) in the depths of my heart. It was a divine, unforgettable experience.

One day I went to Bombay carrying my tin trunk to visit Narayankaka, thinking he would be at home as it was a

Sunday. I had located his Shree Building among the half a dozen buildings at Ghodbunder Road. Two of my uncles were staying there as paying guests on two different floors. As he was still single, Narayankaka had only one outer room for his use. He was taken aback to see me all by myself in the city. Bombay, even in those days, was a big city overflowing with people, and I was barely twelve then. Though Vyankanna was the younger of the two, he was married. When I visited him later, I failed to understand why he took so long to open his door though I kept knocking!

Shree Building was almost like a small township and was occupied by well-off residents engaged in various businesses. Most of them spoke Hindi. Bollywood music director Roshan, comedian Sundar, a Kathak dancer, and several Gujarati merchants lived in the same building. If Sundar returned late at night, his well-built wife would refuse to open the door. He would, then, sleep in our room. My uncles were called Bada (elder) Joshi and Chhota (younger) Joshi by all. Narayankaka was an engineer and had a lucrative job, while Vyankanna was with All India Radio.

Soon I made friends with all my peers in the building. We used to move around Bombay in a BEST bus on a one-rupee ticket. Rakesh Roshan and a Bengali boy also used to join us. Ice cream was priced at just four annas per generous cup and we had a lot of it. The money came, of course, from Narayankaka's wallet. He was generous with me. I sat in a tramcar for the first time in my life, and we could safely hop on and off a moving tram. When sitting on the upper deck of a double-decker bus, reading the signboards of the shops lining the road was a favourite game. However, once while going through a red-light area, we were shaken up by some sights. One of the older boys among us comforted us by saying that there was nothing to be afraid of ... we were passing through the flesh trade market ... that was all.

Since the building housed several people connected with the film world, we often had a chance to sit through shoots. I saw the first day, first show of the popular film *Mr X* in the Lido Talkies. Back in those days, Juhu beach was a clean and quiet spot, with not a single bhelpuri stall in sight. I remember Narayankaka accompanied me for a swim in the sea on an eclipse. On another occasion I even saw, at the Shree Building, the playback luminary Asha Bhosle wearing a white sari and going to Roshan for rehearsing a song.

I never missed a chance to visit Bombay. Narayankaka shifted to Sion. I would consult the daily engagements in the local papers and would dash to see a movie or P.L. Deshpande's show. Bhimanna often gave performances at Matunga and Santacruz, which I attended regularly. Among the most memorable screenings I must include P.L. Deshpande's *Batatyachi Chaal* and *Asa Mi Asami*. I became practically addicted to wandering off to places like the Jehangir Art Gallery to see the beautiful paintings housed there, and to linger in the canteen over a cup of coffee. I simply loved Bombay with its crowd running everywhere, busy people going about their business, homeless people sleeping on the footpaths, people travelling in luxury cars, charming faces flashing on movie hoardings, and so on.

Ramakantkaka of Dharwad often kept me company during my Bombay visits. His father Govindacharya Joshi, Bhimanna's uncle, was a prestigious Kannada publisher. Through his Manohar book series he published excellent literature, including books of most eminent Kannada writers. Ramakantkaka had the task of collecting the library membership fees of Bombay members and also supply them with new books. We used to walk miles on end and occasionally enjoy dosas on the way. I met several Kannada writers while going around with him.

Once while travelling with the writer Yashwant Chittal in his Standard car, in the company of another Kannada writer, there was a heated discussion about a character in S.N. Pendse's Marathi novel *Rathchakra*. I spiritedly participated in this discussion. Everybody was stunned at the reading taste of such a young lad. Despite being Kannad writers, they seemed to appreciate Marathi literature. Their affectionate counsel for me was, 'Raghu, you should also try your hand at writing'. In later years, I became a voracious reader. I finished the volumes of B.M. Purandare's *Raja Shiv Chhatrapati* in one sitting over two days. I had read most of the biographies, magazines, and English novels available in the library. I certainly had an appetite for books.

I was a regular member of the audience whenever Bhimanna performed in Bombay. Once he was performing at Churchgate. During the intermission the 'young prince' climbed into Bhimanna's lap. I was right in front of my father, but he did not so much as look at me. 'She', too, was present. I was so hurt that I got up and sat at the back of the hall, weeping bitterly, unable to understand why I was forsaken, what sin I had committed, especially since Mother had told me how Bhimanna had danced when I was born.

After the performance I waved to him to say that I was leaving. There was no way I could have returned home in the dead of the night. The last local train had already left. I started walking when Bhimanna's student Ramkrishna Patwardhan followed me to say that Bhimanna had asked him to give me a lift home in a taxi. Well, at least one drop of love was spared for me.

The 'young prince' was a pampered brat and it was said that he once broke Bhimanna's tanpura while throwing a tantrum. Sometimes Bhimanna chose to stay with his brother Narayan in Bombay after a performance. Since Narayan was a bachelor, Bhimanna's student Narayan Deshpande also used to stay with him. In due course, Narayankaka got married to Pramilakaku and guests were no longer welcome. Bhimanna would ask him to come to the hotel where he was staying, and Narayankaka would come without fail. He was earning well as he had a degree in metallurgy.

During one such visit he saw a crowd outside Bhimanna's room and on entering he saw the classical dance legend Birju Maharaj and Bhimanna, dressed in vest and pyjamas, with *ghungroo*s (a string of bells), tied on their ankles, rapt in dancing! This continued for an hour. But, of course, Bhimanna was versatile and had excellent rapport with artists in every field.

Once it happened that Bhimanna took the local train after his performance and headed for a friend's house. His friends always considered it a special privilege and favour to host him. He was travelling first class and was alone in the compartment when a miscreant entered, brandished a knife, and demanded money. At the next stop he grabbed hold of the knife with one hand and the man's neck with the other, dragged him to the station master's cabin, and pushed him down to his knees. He was truly fearless. Mother said, 'Your father's neck was so strong that even a knife would give way!'

On one occasion when Bhimanna's guru's anniversary was being celebrated at Kundgol, he was sitting in a room with other artists. Someone was performing on the stage. When his turn was announced, he got up to spit out the paan he was chewing. Someone put his foot forward to trip Bhimanna, who narrowly escaped getting hurt. He said, 'This is unfair. I could have hurt myself. I am to perform now, don't you know?' The cheeky fellow taunted, 'We know what a great singer you are!' Bhimanna went out, cleaned his mouth, came back, and lifted the man off his feet in such a tight grip that he could not breathe and was on the point of fainting. Gangubai Hangal intervened, 'Bhimu, let him go. You'll kill him!' Bhimanna relented and the fellow fell down with a thud. He performed well in the function. He often met with green-eyed jealousy, but showed no weakness anytime, anywhere.

Once while we were still schoolgoing children, he disappeared for almost fifteen days. We had no money, but the grocers kindly allowed us supplies on credit. Meanwhile, my mother received a postcard telling her that he had gone to Kashmir with 'her' and her sisters. Only the rich could afford such luxuries!

Bhimanna was quite gullible and people often swindled him. He once gave me some money to buy cloth and get it stitched by a tailor who was close by. I did so and paid the cloth merchant and the tailor. After about eight days he told me, 'It seems you haven't paid the cloth merchant, so I have paid him now.' I went to the fellow and reminded him that I had paid him and told him that he was a cheat to take money again from Bhimanna. He quietly returned the extra amount.

Whenever Bhimanna returned from his performances I used to enjoy listening to reports of his fine performance as well as stories about him from his friends Dixit, Abhyankar, and Vaidya. One day he had a paan with Vaidya in his bicycle shop, and told him that he was performing in Bombay the next day. Vaidya exclaimed, 'I, too, will be in Bombay tomorrow for some work'. 'Come to the concert after you finish work,' offered Bhimanna, adding, 'we will travel back together in my car'.

The next evening Vaidya, totally soaked in the rain, reached the concert. The doorkeeper would not allow him to enter though he told him that he was Bhimsen's friend. He somehow managed to go up to the entrance and signalled to Bhimanna from there. Bhimanna saw him and announced over the mike, 'He's my friend and has come all this way to listen to me. Allow him in!' Vaidya was ushered to the first row and was even served a cup of hot tea.

'May I begin now?' he asked Vaidya who could not hide his embarrassment. When relating this story, he told me with a lump in his throat, 'I was shivering with cold, but Bhimanna's love and care warmed me up immediately'.

<hr>

Ashwini Kumar, chief of Border Security Force, was a great fan of Bhimanna, and they would often chat over the telephone. Once when he was on duty on the border near Amritsar, Bhimanna took out his car and drove all the way there along with his friends Rajan and Sajan Mishra and their uncle, the sarangi virtuoso Gopal Prasad Mishra. It was the middle of the night when they reached the army post where the guards halted them. 'Connect me to the sahib,' said Bhimanna. 'That cannot be done now. Sahib will not take the call. Come tomorrow morning,' he was told. 'You only have to tell whoever takes the call that Bhimsen has come.' The sentry did so with great reluctance, but was instantly ordered, 'Bring them all here this minute'. The gate was opened and the sentry gave them a crisp salute. Ashwini Kumar was standing at the door to receive them.

After welcoming embraces from all around, the performance began and continued till the break of dawn. Night and day have no relevance to music lovers. Bhimanna recited a poem written by Kumar, who was fluent in English:

The clouds rumbled, the winds zoomed
The flowers blossomed in the garden
Life or death for others, these always bloomed.

Dixit recounted the following incident to me the day after it happened. Bhimanna was driving back after a performance in Bombay, but when he reached the railway crossing at Shivajinagar, Poona, he found the gate was cordoned off by the police. He inquired of a police officer, 'Who's passing by?' The officer paid no attention to him as he was dressed in a simple Nehru shirt, pyjamas, and a jacket. 'Move aside,' Bhimanna was told in the usual stern voice. However, a police constable standing close by recognized him and said, 'Mrs Indira Gandhi is coming'. She was the minister for Information and Broadcasting at that time.

Bhimanna saw his opportunity here and said to his companions, 'Now I will have my way'. The pilot vehicle passed and then came Mrs Gandhi's car. Bhimanna briskly jumped over the cordoning rope and planted himself coolly in the middle of the road. The police immediately surrounded him, but, by now, her car had come close enough for her to see what was happening. She immediately got out of the car, shook hands with Bhimanna, and chatted with him for ten minutes. 'Panditji, it's a long time since I last listened to you. Come to Delhi. I would love to hear something good,' she said as she got back into her car and went away. The rude inspector now turned as soft as putty. Bhimanna said to him, 'No need to panic. But you should know some of the prominent citizens of Poona.' The officer escorted Bhimanna all the way to his house.

At a Sawai Gandharva Sangeet Mahotsav, a young priest with a clean-shaven head and a tuft of hair requested Bhimanna for a free pass, which he gave immediately. Whenever he shook his head in appreciation of Bhimanna's performance, his tuft danced merrily, sending titters of laughter among the young girls sitting behind him. But the festival was known for bringing young people together in blissful companionship!

Five

BHIMANNA RENTED A SPACIOUS flat in Rambaug area on Shastri Road in Poona and moved there. We, too, moved to another residence when I was in the seventh standard. It was a single room where all of us huddled together with Mother, although with a lot of inconvenience. It would get even more crowded when we entertained guests. Mother learnt that a bigger flat with two rooms owned by the Kokil family, her friends, was available on rent. She pestered my father to move us there, to which he did not initially agree. ('She' made sure that not the slightest comfort ever came our way.) Finally since no *pagdi* (deposit money) was asked for and the rent was reasonable, we shifted to the new flat. I was delighted to have such a spacious place now. The front room had a built-in cupboard for our clothes, books, and other sundry objects. I felt enriched by the bounty. We spent happy days in the company of new neighbours and companions.

When I entered matriculation, Bhimanna gave me a new bicycle and a wristwatch. I was in seventh heaven with joy! The municipal commissioner of Bombay had gifted that wristwatch, manufactured by the West End Watch Company in 1945, to Bhimanna. Till this day, I have treasured it. Once he looked in when I was writing an essay in English in black ink on a foolscap paper. 'Is this your handwriting?' he asked.

After a couple of days, he sent a folding table and a chair for my use. This was in appreciation of my neat handwriting. I was elated beyond words.

My matriculation year, 1961–2, is unforgettable for me. School had started in earnest and so had the private tuitions. The daily timetable was stuck on a wall in the house. Every minute from dawn to dusk was marked carefully. I managed to stick to the schedule until the first week of July, but the twelfth day of the month dawned with a calamity that shook the entire city of Poona.

I was in school that day. By the time the first period was over news broke that the Panshet dam had burst and the Mutha river was flooded. We could hardly take in the magnitude of the catastrophe then. However, our school was closed and we were instructed to go home straightaway. I ran home along with my friends. The streets were crowded and my sisters, too, were back home from school. We locked our apartment and moved over to the terrace of a strong concrete building close by. Our building was situated at a higher level so the rising level of water could not touch it, although it was not far from the river. Besides, it was built of clay which would surely have dissolved in the water, and the entire structure would have come toppling down.

We could see from the terrace that Alka Talkies and Sambhaji Bridge had already disappeared under flood water. The satanic mud-red waters had wreaked havoc everywhere on the flat plains. We were dumbstruck with fear.

The water started receding in the afternoon and we returned home. The first whiplash of the floods was felt when electric power failed. The supply of fresh tap water also stopped. We ate our dinner in the dim light of an old lantern and candles.

The next day dawned over a devastated city. Hundreds of people had been killed. Many were saved only because the disaster took place in the morning. Had the dam broken at night, the casualties would have been countless in Poona. I walked around with a few friends to see the state of the city. The riverside roads and lanes were washed away completely. Many houses were razed to the ground. The roads were covered with red mud and tree branches. Pots and pans lay scattered everywhere. The air was filled with the stench of rotting food. One could even see a dead body hanging from the electric wires. Looters and pilferers had a field day.

Our school was closed as it was converted into a relief shelter for the flood-affected. Every new day brought in new difficulties. Drinking water could not be pumped to the higher floors, forcing everybody to carry heavy pots and pitchers from the public supply on the ground floor.

School reopened after a month and studies took off at a terrific speed with extra time being put in to complete the course. My troubles were multiplied as I had to carry water from the ground floor where I picked up my first lessons in 'tap-bickering'. I understood what the idiom 'Many men, many minds' meant. I came into contact with the disciplined and cooperative neighbours as also the selfish and shrewd ones. Women with only a husband to look after would be at the tap for hours, washing pots and clothes. The washing of a doormat took ten minutes! I would look on helplessly with an empty bucket in my hand. Once I lost my patience and threw away their pots and clothes and filled my bucket. It felt perfectly justified as the usual delays had resulted in several cane lashes on my palm from my teacher Mr Athale.

It took several years for Poona to recover from this trauma. Its entire topography underwent a change. New settlements and housing societies rose and the city began to sprawl out in all directions.

∞∞

Bhave Primary School used to host a drama festival in its front yard in those days. I saw most of the classic plays during such festivals. It is difficult to forget the marvellous performances of *Sangeet Manapman*, *Sangeet Soubhadra*, *Vahato Hi Durwanchi Judi*, *To Mee Navhech*, *Ekach Pyala*, and *Tuze Aahe Tujpashi*.

Close to our house stood Bharat Natya Mandir, a theatre where plays were performed regularly. Sometimes Bhimanna would also be seen among the audience. He would be the chief invitee at musical performances. This used to be quite a trying time for the performers, but he showered unstinting praise on the talented artists.

The folk play *Radhabai Budhgaonkar* was to be performed at this theatre. I was curious to see what a tamasha was like. The Krishna–Pendya dialogue started and when the corpulent Radhabai came on stage, the dancing boy shouted, 'Come, come, come, a little steadily, slowly....'

To this Radhabai answered, 'Oh you dead one, why should I come slowly?' (Laughter in the theatre.)

'No, no, madam, I just meant, sit down slowly....'

'And if I don't sit down slowly?' asked Radhabai.

'You might crush this lamb under your weight,' answered the dancing boy. (The audience burst into resounding laughter.)

Then the repartee between Krishna and Pendya began.

'Why are our maids staring in front today? Is there any special presence here?'

Pendya answered, 'My God, don't you see that Bhimsen Joshi—whose maddening notes compete with your flute—is sitting in front of us?'

Thunderous clapping broke out in the theatre and I saw Bhimanna sitting in the front row. I quickly sneaked out of the place. Bhimanna did not have an exclusivist approach to the other art forms. He made it a point to witness good films too.

I thoroughly enjoyed the school vacation with visits to the theatre thrice a day, an occasional jump into the swimming pool, hours of cricket on the S.P. College grounds under the scorching sun, and assaulting my opponents with the cricket bat for a wrong decision. How quickly the vacation ended! But at the end, when the results came, I passed with flying colours.

Sometimes Narayankaka and Vyankanna would drop in on their way to Bombay, bringing us a variety of sweetmeats. If Bhimanna were present the talk would go back to old times. A deep intimacy could be seen between them. They adored him: he was, after all, their elder brother. Narayankaka would affectionately refer to him as 'our Dharmaraj', the magnanimous character from the Mahabharata. Vyankanna had a great sense of humour, and was fond of telling stories. One such story was about a husband and a wife. He would narrate how once one could hear the sound of a beating from behind the closed door of the couple's house. The husband shouted, 'How dare you do this?' His words were followed by the sound of a blow. Eventually when the door opened, a dejected husband stepped out: it was he who had received the bashing at the hands of his wife! We enjoyed listening to Vyankanna's stories.

To fight her loneliness, Mother joined Sevasadan School to learn Marathi. She completed her studies till the final year and enrolled for matriculation with me. However, she could not find time to study as she was expecting her fourth child, my brother Anand. That was the end of her education. Though herself in deep suffering, Mother made many friends in those days and helped several women like Mrs Hirwate.

Once when she came to know that the wife of a Marathi film actor had refused to pay her maid, Mother took up the cause and told the woman, 'Don't be proud because your husband is a star. My husband, too, is world-famous, but we don't loot the poor. This is unjust. Pay the maid right away.' The poor soul got her salary the next day. Mother wiped the tears of others although she herself wept day in and day out: this showed her generous nature.

Mother formed lifelong friendships with many women from good families, such as Ambu Deshpande, Mrs Vaidya, Chhaya Kulkarni, Mrs Koshe (Professor Koshe's wife), and Mrs Kulkarni who lived near Shaniwar Wada. Also there was Kari Aunty or Sanni Aunty (which, in Kannada means younger aunt), Mother's friend from the Gadag days. Her children, Manda, Mukund, and Nandu, belonged to our age group and we were like siblings. We called her husband Bhau (brother). He was affectionate and often asked us to stay with them. They lived in the cantonment area behind the Poona railway station. Coming as we did from the middle-class Brahminical Sadashiv Peth, we could easily distinguish ourselves from their Anglo-Indian lifestyle. Sadashiv Peth let out the aroma of *sabudana khichdi* (sago khichri), while the cantonment side smelt of crisp omelettes. Manda did her matriculation with me. Later she married into the industrialist Bandekar family of Goa. Mukund settled down comfortably in Dubai. Manda and Mukund travelled in Mercedes cars in those days, but always showered love and affection on Mother and us. They were a great support to Mother.

Our two homes—Mother and we in one place and the 'others' in another—presented a study in contrast. It was all luxury for them, while it was deprivation, dishonour, and dejection for us. The 'others' tried to reduce us to nonentities in the community. We were children disowned by our own father and a wife abandoned by her own husband. In the course of time 'they' began to refer to themselves as 'Bhimsen's family', totally eclipsing us, the real family. Quarrels became routine between Bhimanna and Mother. I was convinced that a shrewd, heartless person had led him into temptations.

Bhimanna's visits to us were slowly decreasing. Whenever I had to approach him for money for monthly expenses, 'she' used to question me closely about the particulars. Now that I was sufficiently grown-up to understand the whole state of affairs, I would sometimes argue over it. We were deprived of the prestige, luxury, and comfort enjoyed by the 'other' family. So much so that at times after Bhimanna's concert was over and I would be walking back home from the Lakshmi Krida Mandir Hall, his Buick car would pass me by. He would certainly see me walking, but he would never give me a lift if 'she' was sitting by his side. Dr Nanasaheb Deshpande, who would also be passing by in his Hillman car, disapproved of this behaviour and would stop to give me a lift to my house. These occasional touches of humanity often comforted us in those days of humiliation.

Bhimanna was like a lion, but he was saddened by the bickering between his two families and the pricks of his conscience. His drinking bouts were on the increase. He would simply go missing for a few days when touring out of the town for a performance. Obviously he could not ride two horses, nor be a part of two families at the same time. 'She' was totally opposed to allowing him his freedom.[1]

One evening in 1963, Dr Nanasaheb Deshpande dropped in at our place when I was studying in pre-degree class. He told us that Bhimanna had taken seriously ill in Hyderabad. I immediately rushed to Secunderabad, where Bandukaka was living and working as a railway guard. I searched out his address, bathed at his place, and rushed to the hospital where Bhimanna was diagnosed with gastroenteritis. The doctor assured me that he was out of danger. He was Bhimanna's fan and had looked after him with great diligence. In fact, I was told that he had stayed with Bhimanna throughout the night.

Bhimanna was sleeping when I entered the room. There was a riot of painful feelings in my heart. I thought that when he opens his eyes I should tell him, 'Give your wealth to *them*, but give me your music', like Arjuna, who, when given the choice by Krishna between himself and his armies, chose Krishna. I was, of course, too shy to say this when he woke up and cast a glance at me. 'How did you know?' he asked. But before I began my story 'she' entered and was enraged to see me present there. I quickly made my exit.

The next day when he was moved to the residence of a friend, Mr Potdar, I went to see him. Again 'she' raised an objection to my presence. Bhimanna was too weak to speak. He simply gestured to Bandukaka, who asked me to stay over with him, and I was eventually sent back to Poona.

In an obituary, a sycophant described 'her' as 'the very image of kindness'. I do not know whether he had the same words for his own mother. However, it was a good joke!

Soon after Bhimanna was operated on for sinus trouble by Dr Atre at his hospital in the Hirabaug area of Poona. He decided to perform the surgery without anaesthesia as he did not wish to damage Bhimanna's vocal cords. For this the palate had to be perforated, a very painful procedure. Bhimanna was blindfolded, but he saw the whole procedure by removing it. A few friends, including Dr Deshpande and Dixit, came to see him. When he was brought out on a stretcher he remarked, 'This is how they have arranged my funeral'. This evoked only weak laughter. I, too, was standing in a corner. The doctor had warned Bhimanna against chewing tobacco for a few days. Even so, the moment he was wheeled into his private room, he stuffed a ball of tobacco into his mouth. Just then the doctor chanced to enter. 'What is this, Anna!' he exclaimed. Bhimanna answered, 'I have put the tobacco on the other side of the mouth, away from where you performed the surgery!'

After my pre-degree examination, I decided to go to Gadag by myself, and I reached at ten in the night. My grandfather Bandekaka was the station master; a coolie escorted me with my luggage to his bungalow. He was a strict disciplinarian, but was known for being just. Ramakantkaka once told me an interesting story about him which I remembered then.

Bandekaka's uncle, Raghavendra Acharya, also a station master, was once performing puja in his railway quarters when a goods train halted at the station. A passenger train was following it on the same track, but he would never dream of leaving his puja halfway. His assistant, who minded the signal, was not available either. Bandekaka was then just a student studying in the seventh standard. Realizing the danger, he changed the signal, got the goods train out of the way, and made room for the incoming passenger train. An English officer, who was travelling by the train, noted what this young kid had done. He sent for the boy, gave him an appointment letter on the spot, and got him to join the railways. Bandekaka—the kid—had not done even his matriculation then!

Bandekaka was a man of discipline, but he was kind-hearted too. Once when the signalman did not give a quick signal to a train, the driver got down and slapped the signalman. By the time Bandekaka became aware of this, the train had already departed. He asked the signalman not to give a green signal when the same train returned in the evening. When the signal was delayed again in the evening, as directed, the driver got down in a fit of rage and shouted, 'Where is the station master?' Someone pointed to the cabin and the angry driver rushed in. Bandekaka was going about his work unperturbed, and the signalman was standing meekly in a corner. When the driver entered the cabin, Bandekaka gestured to the man to close the door. The driver was visibly shaken. The signalman asked Bandekaka, 'What next, sir?' 'Give him two tight slaps,' said Bandekaka, and the signalman did just that. The matter was thus settled equitably and without any argument.

Bandekaka's hospitality evoked admiration all around. He arranged a special bogie for the cast of Bhimanna's play *Bhagyashree* all the way from Hubli, and that too without putting any particulars on record. When the train reached Mundhwa station near Poona, he purchased thirty-five tickets, disconnected the special bogie, and accommodated the whole cast in another compartment. The same arrangement was made for the return journey. The players were served hot tea and vadas at every station the train crossed, as were the driver and the conductor-guard!

That was Grandfather Bandekaka! When he saw me standing at his door at such an odd hour of the night, he only said, 'It's quite dark now. Have something to eat and stay over with us tonight. You can go to see Guranna tomorrow.' So I stayed at his place. His children, though younger than me, were uncle and aunt to me by relation. Bandekaka had remarried after his first wife had died and these were the children from his second marriage. They enjoyed our conversations. The Joshi family was blessed with many sons, but only a few daughters. As a result, girls were his favourites and they had the same pet names in all branches of the family. Just like my Dummi Aunty, there was a 'Dummi' in Bandekaka's house too.

The next morning I moved to my grandfather's place. As I bowed before him he said, 'It's a day of fasting today. Wash yourself.' By the time I had bathed, he had completed his morning puja. He was wearing a coarse loincloth. He was fair-complexioned, and his hairy body and arms as well as his forehead were smeared with stripes of sandalwood paste. His clean-shaven head showed a tuft. My uncle was busy laying the plates for food. All of Grandmother Godabai's children were younger than me. Grandfather chanted the prayer *Venkatramana Govinda* and poured holy water into our mouths. Food was offered to the gods before we started eating. We had never eaten so early and in this style in Poona. This, however, was a way of life here. Grandfather himself generously served mango juice brought from Ningadhalli, and Grandmother Godabai poured pure ghee on it. When my grandfather came to me I saw a smile on his lips, but tears in his eyes. An important reason behind my Gadag visit was to meet Great-Grandmother Ambakka who lived with my grandfather. She cuddled me with great affection, made me sit close to her and said, 'Bhimu's elder son? God bless you with a long life.' On the way back I stayed overnight with Ram Mama (Ram Katti) in Hubli.

One evening I went to see Bhimanna at his house in Rambaug. Clad in a lungi and a vest, he was tinkering with his Buick. 'Good that you are here! Hold this.' He placed in my hand an imported car-part, which he was trying to fit in the Delco section. It was a delicate job with small screws to be fitted in, but the part would not stay put and fell off each time he tried to fix it in. I held a flashlight as it had become dark by then. After an hour's efforts, he finally succeeded. He put a ball of tobacco into his mouth and asked me to focus on the spot. He held the feeler gauge over the bonnet and began to adjust the gap. It was done at last! He slapped me on the back with great happiness as the engine began to work smoothly. I never rode in it, but this happy occasion when he and I worked together is an indelible memory.

I have no words to describe Bhimanna's driving skills. He would drive his well-maintained car all the way from Calcutta to Bombay, dressed in shorts and a vest and wearing his Ray-Ban sunglasses. After which he would wash himself in cold water and give a four-hour-long concert. The concert over, he would drive all the way to Poona.

His friend Dixit once narrated to me an example of Bhimanna's expertise in car engineering. After his concert at Walchandnagar, Bhimanna was returning to Poona with a driver in a car belonging to the sethji. The car stopped half-way about twenty-five or thirty miles from Poona. It was early morning and Bhimanna was fast asleep. The driver began to tinker with the engine, but in vain. The car would not start. Eventually he said, 'Sahib, we have to wait for another vehicle.'

Bhimanna got down from the car and asked the driver to open the bonnet, which the man did unwillingly. Bhimanna looked closely at the engine and asked him to look around for a piece of silver foil from a disposed cigarette packet on the road. Bhimanna wrapped the foil around the fuse and fixed it back in place. The engine started turning immediately. When the journey was resumed, he asked the driver, 'How long have you been driving a car?' 'Ten years, Sahib,' he replied. 'How come you do not know such a simple trick? If a job is worth doing, then learn to do it well.' The driver nodded humbly to Bhimanna.

∞⧢∞

As I have said before, when I was studying in college there used to be frequent bickering over money between Bhimanna and me. He gave ridiculous excuses for not paying me. 'I cannot meet with my own expenses.' 'I have to pay heavy income tax.' And so forth. I would then argue, 'Your income is high, therefore your taxes are high. Give us a slightly bigger share from that high income of yours.' (All this time, however, the 'other' family was living in the lap of luxury.) Sometimes he would go to the extreme and shout, 'This is my money. I will squander it the way I choose. It is none of your business.' This would devastate me. I knew that these were not his words; they had been implanted into him. His simple formula was, 'Sing as much as you can, do what you like, and leave money matters to others'. That was the typical impractical Tukaram attitude.

Purushottam Walawalkar, Bal Gandharva's harmonium accompanist, once talked about his maestro's 'weakness': once he placed his trust in any person he would never bother to question it, even if he knew it was misplaced. In my opinion, a divine voice and a credulous nature were two qualities shared by these two maestros. Bhimanna was like the gullible Shiva who gave his blessing even to the devil who pleased him.

It once happened that Bhimanna did not return from Bombay for four days. When I went to the 'other' house to inquire, I saw that my stepbrother was preparing to leave for Bombay in search of our father. Most unexpectedly 'she' agreed that I should accompany him as Bhimanna was sure to accede to my request to return home, I being the eldest son.

My stepbrother knew most of the addresses of Bhimanna's friends as he had frequently visited the city. We looked for him at Mr Mhatre of Mhatre Industries. He was not there. We moved on to other places. During the search he kept complaining about Bhimanna's frequently whimsical and wayward behaviour and his failure to bring home money. We found Bhimanna at the house of a VIP, but he was in no mood to talk with us as he was inebriated. He would often get moody and would be beyond all reasoning. Finally we persuaded a reluctant Bhimanna to return with us. A taxi was booked and we drove to stage actor Dr Kashinath Ghanekar's house. On the way, he stopped the taxi and telephoned the doctor's house for a car. His wife answered the bell, opened the door, handed over the keys of the car to us, and said, 'He is unwell'. Then the door was closed. Obviously, she wanted to keep her husband away from another tippler.

Bhimanna got behind the steering wheel, but the engine refused to start. We gave it a push-start and hopped in. He halted in front of a house in Matunga, got down, and started to climb its staircase. A dark Konkani woman opened the door. He spoke to her in Konkani. She handed some bottles of home-made liquor to him and implored, 'Brother, don't drink so much'. We push-started the car again and drove towards Poona.

A little after Bandra, Bhimanna suddenly changed lanes. On being asked why he had done so he said, 'Behind us is a big vehicle being driven fast; the man does not know that there is a road divider ahead. He might bump straight into us.' That is precisely what happened, but the situation was saved as the other driver saw the divider just in time and took a sharp turn to avoid it. It was amazing that despite being inebriated Bhimanna's driving skills remained exemplary. Meanwhile, I poured all the liquor on to the road without Bhimanna realizing it. However, at the very next traffic signal, he noticed what I had done, scolded me, and took a U-turn to go back to the same house. He brooked no interference in his planning.

I don't recall where we spent the night. He was in no mood to return to Poona. We whiled away our time till noon and went to a theatre in Dadar where a matinee show of Arun Sarnaik's play was on. 'Look at that sworn enemy of mine, scowling at us,' said Bhimanna, pointing to a man who was looking angrily at him. He would never behave like that with anybody. We went to the green room after the first act. Arun Sarnaik was greatly pleased to see Bhimanna there. 'We're honoured,' he said. With him stood the child actor Sachin, who was also Bhimanna's fan. We had a short chat with them and then resumed our journey.

After repeated imploring we finally came to the airport. A friend of his had already purchased the tickets. As we were entering the building Mukundrao Kirloskar, the editor of *Kirloskar* magazine, came running to us. He said that he, too, wanted to go to Poona, but tickets were not available. Bhimanna arranged for his ticket and we boarded the plane which took off fifteen minutes late on account of all this to-do.

Once on the plane, Bhimanna insisted on going to the cockpit where the pilot turned out to be his fan. I, too, was called in to have a look. Bhimanna pointed at one spot and asked the pilot, 'Is a part missing here?' The pilot was stumped, for there was a visible difference in the spot of that particular part. Bhimanna certainly had a keen eye for mechanical structures. That was my first and only air travel with Bhimanna. The next time I travelled by air was thirty years later, on a visit to Udaipur, after an improvement in my fortunes.

On reaching Poona we did not go straight home, but went to veteran writer Vyankatesh Madgulkar's bungalow. After a little chat there, my stepbrother was asked to sing a song, which he did well. I stood unnoticed in a corner. Bhimanna knew that I too could sing well, however, I belonged to the persona non grata family, after all.

I visited the 'other' home the next day when 'she', Bhimanna, and his friend Dixit happened to be arguing hotly. 'She' was reading him a lecture. 'This is how he behaves,' said she to Dixit. 'I am here for his music and under his shelter. How can he go on like this?' For a moment Bhimanna forgot that I was also present standing in one corner, and he shouted at her, 'I know what you are here for. You are getting money all right. Enough of this drama.'

That was enough for me too and I slunk away. Once I ventured to suggest to 'her' to let Bhimanna occasionally enjoy a drink or two at home so that he would not run away. 'After all, he is an artist,' I added, whereupon 'she' snapped, 'That's all nonsense! This is business.' That was music to my ear.

While in Bombay, Bhimanna once took us to the Goa Hindu Association Theatre. He had composed music for their play *Dhanya Tegayani Kala*. The singer Ramdas Kamat was practising the song '*Dhan dhan bhag suhag tero*' composed in raga Kalashree by Bhimanna. I was all ears. I came out and stood in the gallery where the harmonium maestro Thakurdas was present.

It was evening and I sang raga Marwa for about fifteen minutes. Thakurdasji was pleased and patted me. He went in and said, 'Raghu crooned Marwa quite well just now', to Bhimanna, who looked at me with great affection. In his heart of hearts he was aware of the inheritance he had handed over to me. Marwa is a forte of the Kirana Gharana and performing it to suit a special mood poses a big challenge. Bhimanna also composed one more song in raga Lalit Bhatiyar for the same play. He often sang the composition '*Dhan dhan mangal gao*' (Let us sing for good fortune) in raga Kalashree in his concerts as well.

Bhimanna once borrowed his brother Narayan's Ambassador car to return to Poona. On the way, with his usual generosity, he tipped the waiter, who served us tea, 100 rupees. The car was not in good condition and gave us trouble in the ghats. On reaching Poona Bhimanna sent the car to the garage, got it fixed, filled the tank, and sent it back to his brother in Bombay. Then he took us in a taxi to Vinod Doshi's factory on the Poona–Bombay road. Mr Doshi, who greatly admired Bhimanna, sent back the taxi, cancelled his own engagements, and requested Bhimanna to have a meal with him in his luxurious bungalow. Hot bhakris, Bhimanna's favourite dish, were served with a sizzling tadka poured on them. 'Anna, you live a rich and melodious life, indeed! Ours is a dry existence.' That, of course, was with reference to Bhimanna's music.

During my first year of college, Bhimanna once came to our place at eleven in the night. All the others had gone to Karnataka to attend a wedding, leaving me behind as my classes were on. I was just going to have dinner, and asked him whether he would like to eat. 'I'll go to bed.' Saying this he took off his shirt and lay on the cot. Immediately I started pressing his feet, which was a family practice—a touch says more than words. Since he had to sing sitting cross-legged, he always suffered from aching legs. He then motioned me to stop, and I began to give him a head massage. I really used to enjoy touching his thick, black, curly mop. Mother often used to remark, 'In his youth, your father looked like Madan.' Then he said, 'Sleep here. Close to me.' And I snuggled up to him. He asked me in a soft voice, 'Which is your favourite raga?' 'Malkauns,' I replied. And he began to sing it.

It was only for me, me alone. I could feel the vibrations of his breath and notes. I was filled with joy, as if I were right at the very source from where Malkauns rose. Again in the early morning I woke up to the tender and soft notes of Asawari Todi. And again I reached a state of bliss. Bhimanna left early in the morning. What was left behind in my memory was his sweet rendering and the faint scent of his clothes.

I was once told by some of his friends that it was around this time that Bhimanna tried to commit suicide. Nadkarni in his biography has dropped a hint to that effect.

❧

If I stayed late in college on account of having to complete my practicals, Mother would go to the 'other' house. Once on my return I found her weeping sorely. She had been taunted and insulted by 'her', while Bhimanna had remained a passive spectator. (I recalled the scene in a film on Picasso's life where he continues to paint undisturbed while his two wives quarrel with each other.)

'Her' children, too, would join in the slanging session. Once Mother was told, 'Woman, don't show your face here anymore'. I was furious when I heard this and I went to the 'other' house where Bhimanna, too, was present. I asked him, 'Why should they speak so rudely to my mother? Ask them to keep in mind their age and my mother's age too.' Suddenly the children rushed out at me and shouted, 'We will not put up with your mother's insulting words to our mother'. I said, 'The user knows where the shoe pinches. I have never insulted your mother. We all are only children and have no business meddling in the affairs of elders. Mind you, I will not tolerate such behaviour anymore.'

Even so they would never let go a chance to revile Mother. Then she, too, would retaliate spiritedly, 'Mine is a legitimately solemnized marriage. I am not a runaway like you. Be warned, God knows everything.' This was sharp enough to hurt 'her'. Then 'she', too, would retort, 'A crow's curses can't kill a cow!'

The days following such verbal clashes used to be very upsetting for us. The 'others', however, were totally unaffected. In fact, they seemed to enjoy these fights. When Bhimanna kept total silence during such encounters, I used to get very angry and once even told him off, 'You have become a slave to a tyrant!' Whenever his fees for his performances were paid to him 'she' would grab it all. He was not left with even a single pie to buy his tobacco. One of the students of Hirabai Barodekar—the renowned musician—said to me once that Bhimanna told her that he was not really such a monster. He was helpless; the moment he reached home, they snatched away all his earnings.

My younger brother Anand was born when I was doing my matriculation. Bhimanna was now, as it were, put under house arrest, making it impossible for him to visit us. Even so, he would give 'her' the slip occasionally and continue to visit us. A neighbour called Shamrao always invited Bhimanna to his place whenever he came to us. The book *Bhimsen* enlightened me on all these happenings later on. It turned out that this man was a spy reporting Bhimanna's whereabouts to 'her'. He called himself her *gurubandhu* (pupil of the same guru)! Naturally, he had a free entry to Bhimanna's concerts. Meanwhile, a second son was born to 'her' too!

My brother Anand had a congenital defect in his feet. Mother used to take him to Dr Motwani for treatment. The newborn in the other house was stricken with polio. I remember meeting Bhimanna and the 'others' in a hospital located opposite the Chhatrapati Sambhaji Garden.

After having used several sedans, Bhimanna settled for a Fiat and continued to drive miles on end to perform at various places. Abasaheb Garware had a great affection for him and he presented his Impala to him. However, the car turned out to be a white elephant and consumed gallons of petrol which Bhimanna could not afford. He returned the vehicle to Abasaheb. Bhimanna's reputation had by now crossed all national borders and there was no musical conference of significance in the country where Bhimanna was not performing.

Professor Marathe's math tuition class being over, I was leaving for home when he called out to me. 'You are Bhimsen Joshi's son, aren't you?' 'Yes, sir,' I replied. 'Today's *Times* carries a laudatory write-up on him. I don't have much of a musical ear, but I am his admirer. I am curious about your father's source of livelihood.' I told him that Bhimanna did not have to do any job as his fees were enough to keep him in a financial position. However, he was not satisfied with this answer and continued, 'But how much does he earn for each performance?'

I told him, 'On an average, Bhimanna gives about nine to ten performances every month at the rate of about three thousand per performance.' That stunned him.

A lot of ignorance prevails even among the knowledgeable about the esteem in which artistes are held.

I passed my Inter-Science Examination with good credits, but it was not enough to get me a seat in an engineering college in Poona. Another option was a seat at the Walchand College of Engineering, Sangli. I went to Bhimanna with a request to send me there for my engineering degree. But he replied, 'I cannot afford your lodging and boarding expenses there'. Obviously this response was prompted by 'her'. Eventually I enrolled for a BSc degree from Poona. All this while the other household was enjoying the fruits of Bhimanna's prosperity. Nevertheless, he continued to pay my fees and give me some pocket money too.

At this time food rationing was introduced, and items like sugar, grains, and ghee could be procured from the ration shops. The festival of Diwali was around the corner and a special quota of rations had been released. Since I had to attend classes in college, Mother stood in the long queue before the ration shop. An acquaintance turned to her in surprise and remarked, 'How come you are in this queue? This same shopkeeper had sent a full can of pure ghee to the 'other' house. Mother broke into tears.

I often questioned Bhimanna why he practised such discrimination. There was no response. 'Money is not everything. Human beings need love and care too,' I told him. This, too, went in through one ear and came out of the other. It was clear that we could have no share in his success and affluence. We were all growing up, but we had to be satisfied with whatever was doled out to us.

During my college days a Marathi movie *Mee Tulas Tujhya Angani* had been rereleased in a local theatre. It was based on the life of an artist and Bhimanna had sung a lot of songs for it. I liked the movie mainly for his playback singing. Morning ragas combined with excellent photography added to the total effect. In the *jugalbandi* (simultaneous performance) *'Ketki gulab juhi champak ban phule'* (So many flowers are blooming in the garden ushering in spring) from the movie *Basant Bahar*, set in raga Basant, Bhimanna and Manna Dey, the eminent Hindi playback singer, reached the very summit of their performances. Around that time, Bhimanna also sang the *abhang* (devotional songs sung in verse form) *'Indrayani kaathi devachi aalandi'* in P.L. Deshpande's Marathi movie *Gulacha Ganapati*. The audience never felt tired of listening to the song in every concert of Bhimanna, as he would sing it for half an hour at a time.

I was a shy boy then and never pushed myself into the limelight anywhere, whether in conversation or in singing. My friend Dilip Thatte got me associated with a students' union. I was given the responsibility of escorting the chief guests at various programmes. This gave me a chance to meet with some celebrities and to get to know them well.

The celebrated writer N.S. Phadke liked to have a clean tablecloth with a jug of drinking water and a glass in front of him. When I went to the critic S.K. Kshirsagar's house he was sitting in a chair with piles of books all around him. He was shaving and had worked up a thick lather. He looked at me and said, 'You have come long before time. Sit down on the cot there.' I moved aside some books and sat down.

Halfway through the shaving he asked me my name. When I told him, he turned around and asked, 'Are you Bhimsen Joshi's son?' Then he started inquiring about Bhimanna, his father, and the Joshi family's native place. While answering his queries, I was looking at the lather drying up on half his face and the razor in his hand, and thought what if our chief guest were to cut himself with it! At that moment, the cab driver sounded the horn and I took my chance to exit and wait downstairs for him.

There were girls, too, in the union and clean friendships made it easy to conduct various activities, though some of the other students looked at our gatherings with suspicion. I was known by the name 'Rabhi'.

The union once convened a national meet in which students from the northeast regions like Nagaland and Manipur were also invited. The intention was to forge some kind of national integration through close interaction and cultural exchange. The students were accommodated in the houses of willing hosts in the city. One of the girls from Manipur, Shakuntala, was put up with Mr Vaidya, the owner of the Swastik Rubber Factory, and I was asked to escort her around.

All activities would take place strictly as per schedule. Once when I went to pick up the girl, Mrs Vaidya gave us a lift in her luxury car. She asked the driver to take a detour to Deccan Gymkhana where she stopped the car in front of the Bata shoe shop. She asked the girl to buy whatever she wanted, paid for it, and dropped us at our venue. The girl was pleased with this unexpected gift.

Shakuntala came from a well-to-do family and looked charming with her fair complexion and gazelle eyes. She could easily belong to any of the typical Konkanasth Brahmin families of Poona. After all the programmes were over, I took her in an autorickshaw to her host's place. We had hardly spent four days together, yet she seemed sad at the parting. I saw tears shining in her eyes. I, too, was moved when I said, 'Come again'.

The entire experience, however, made me a little bolder. My friend Dilip Thatte even told me that he could see a marked difference in my deportment now that the tense expression on my face had vanished. It could be that the stressful relationship between our two homes had put it there. After all self-knowledge takes its own time to bloom. As ill luck would have it, this good friend died prematurely of cancer.

I have read R.V. Dighe's *Gaanlubdha Mrugnayana*, a historical novel about the love between two music lovers. It showed how gazelle-eyed girls were easy prey to music and musicians. There must have been several such gazelle-eyed damsels cavorting around Bhimanna, too, but he never lost his poise. One of his friends once remarked to me, 'Your father is a great man, an excellent man. Many garlands await the necks of such great men.'

Whenever Bhimanna gave a concert in Poona, I was sure to be present there. Some people did not like my presence. I would wait at the door for him to come. When he saw me standing there, he would gesture to me to enter along with him, and I would follow suit. Those who obstructed my entry only earned for themselves a name for being mean-minded. Once a man asked me to prove that Bhimanna was my father. I simply told him that in our country no one ever takes one's father name falsely. At that very moment, a favourite student of Bhimanna came up and prevented the situation from escalating.

I started buying tickets to Bhimanna's concerts when I started earning. The joy I felt now was greater than the grief I had had to suffer earlier. As soon as the concert was over I would approach Bhimanna, touch his feet, and leave. If 'she' were not around he would have a few words with me, otherwise he would simply nod in acknowledgement.

Once at the conclusion of a performance, my friend Jayant Badve asked Bhimanna the name of the raga. After the people had left he turned to Jayant and said, 'Do you try to get the horoscope of the girl you like in college? First, learn to appreciate her beauty. Enjoy music, listen intently. Ask questions only when you decide to marry!' The hall resounded with laughter.

~

1. Mohan Nadkarni has particularly mentioned this situation in his book *Bhimsen Joshi: A Biography* (New Delhi: HarperCollins, 1983).

Six

BHIMANNA WAS VERY HEALTH CONSCIOUS in those days. He bathed twice a day in cold water in all seasons. He was moderate in his eating habits, and would never eat unless he was hungry. The only exceptions were paan, tobacco, and tea. He could drink any number of cups of tea at any hour of the day. He liked to chew white betel nut, which he continued till the end. He had strong dentures. When I asked why he consumed so much tobacco, his explanation was that all singers did so because paan and tobacco cleanse the throat. Since he had to eat out several times a month, he would regularly deworm himself and use laxatives, such as the herbal supplement Isabgol with milk. After the age of sixty, he started eating Threptin biscuits as a protein supplement.

He tuned every cell in his body in the same way a musician tunes the strings of his instrument. It gave him full control over his body. As a result whenever he ascended the platform for a performance, it was as if his entire physique were primed to perform. The movements of his fingers, his eyes, and his head manifested this total absorption of music in his body. His audience was also then drawn into the full musical experience. Such health consciousness is an example to be emulated by young artists who want to have total control over their bodies.

Whenever he returned from a concert out of Poona, he would ask a masseur to give him a vigorous *maalish* (massage).

A body exhausted after a four-hour performance and an equally long drive deserved such relaxation. He had total command over sleep—he could as easily enter a deep sleep whenever he wanted as he could forgo it for three days at a stretch. I consider this to be a yogic power.

Dr N. Sheshagiri, Pramilakaku's brother, was a noted scientist. He had yogic abilities too. He once told me, 'Raghu, we regard your father as a yogi. All the circles—chakras—described in yoga, from the throat to the navel, are active in him. That is why his notes are burnished by the Sun Chakra and are, therefore, sublime, ineffable. They defy all comparison. That is why when they are uttered, a singular joy emanates from them for all.' Narayankaka had also told me that the headstrong cow at Gadag would turn extremely docile while being milked when Bhimanna was practising.

Bhimanna's singing had the same kind of fragrance that pure home-made ghee emanates. I have stored it in my heart. I have understood the secret of expressing emotions in singing and cannot put up with any lesser performance by any other vocalist, howsoever great he may be.

He was the personification of cleanliness. He shaved every day. If he saw me unshaved for a day, he would immediately rebuke me. He also liked clean, spick-and-span clothes. I have even seen him sweep the house. Once I saw him sitting quietly with a wet face; when I asked him the reason he said, 'Wetting the face is like a tanner soaking a piece of leather. I shave when the skin becomes soft.' Whenever he returned from his (frequent) hospitalizations, a domestic help shaved him. I had presented him with a new razor. When I met him the next day he remarked jocularly, 'Well, you have shaved me clean.'

He liked the colour white. It suited him for he himself was like the dazzling sun. All the objects and gadgets that he used were kept in top condition. His BSA bicycle was a shining model of excellent upkeep. So was his car, clean inside out.

He was fond of high-quality Kannauj attars, which the merchants from the north regularly supplied to him. 'Kanta' and 'Priya' were his favourites. He liked to wear flat wrist-watches. In the course of time he started wearing rings with expensive precious stones. Both his notes and his diamonds shone equally brightly in the concerts.

He always kept with him a silver paan box with Ganapati engraved on its lid. It contained a mix of excellent quality cardamoms, cloves, and white betel-nut pieces. I used to enjoy them occasionally. All doctors chew at least two cloves a day, he told me. Of course, he chewed at least a dozen every day. He also kept some Ibrah zarda (tobacco) and lime paste in the box. He purchased it from Suratwala, the only dealer in Poona, and would stock a couple of months' supply. As an interesting coincidence, Suratwala's granddaughter Leena became my daughter-in-law, thereby sealing this tobacco relationship permanently!

He often visited the main vegetable *mandi* (market) to purchase betel leaves. His fans there would line up before him whispering 'Panditji is here', and touch his feet. He knew many of them by name and acknowledged their affection with a smile. They called him 'Maauli', meaning mother. That is also how the great saint Dnyaneshwar was called by his devotees. There can hardly be a more appropriate description of this yogi of music who has rendered several melodious bhajans in Marathi and Kannada. Whenever I visited Karnataka, I bought large quantities of betel leaves for him.

He ate well and properly. He enjoyed bread and butter for breakfast. He drank milk out of a giant-sized mug, half a litre at a time. His main meal included his favourite jowar rotis, fresh home-made butter, and green vegetables. Curds were always welcome, and chapattis made with a filling of jaggery were a feast for him. He ate a lot of fruits, especially figs, *chiku*s, bananas, and papayas. He enjoyed dishes like onion bhaji and chilli bhaji, while an all-time favourite was the Karnataka-style poha chivda.

When I was a schoolgoing boy I had heard that Dr Shridhar Ketkar, the chief editor of *Maharashtriya Jnanakosha*, the first-ever encyclopaedia in Marathi, used to carry onion bhaji in his pocket! I had seen Bhimanna, too, regularly carrying a paper bag full of poha in his pocket and eating from it.

I discovered the secret of his preference for poha chivda, the basic ingredient of both being poha (flattened rice), which contains a good supply of carbohydrates. Chivda, supported by high proteins in peanuts and gram makes for a tasty, dry snack. Poha, freshly made, and enriched by Bhimanna with half a dozen green chillies to include vitamin C—as recommended by Dr H.V. Sardesai—with raw onion added to it, is a healthy, complete food.

He derived the same quality of happiness from this combination as from a good performance at a concert. However, as said before, he never ate unless he was hungry.

Bhimanna was a polyglot with good command over Marathi, Kannada, English, Hindi, Konkani, Urdu, and even Punjabi, especially the slang. Pandit Rajan Mishra narrated the following episode. Once when he was travelling by a horse carriage in Punjab, singing all the way, the driver picked up a quarrel and used swear words. Bhimanna got down, pulled him out, dealt a resounding slap across his face, and used the same language for him. A crowd gathered, among whom many recognized Bhimanna and a thorough bashing was showered on the ill-mannered man. He touched Bhimanna's feet and Bhimanna invited him to his concert due at night.

Bhimanna had a photographic memory and could readily place anyone even after a passage of fifteen years, remember his name, and even when and where he had met him. He knew all the towns, streets, and roads in the country like the lines on his palms. He could recall any telephone number even if he had dialled it only once. The number plates of his friends' cars were on the tip of his tongue. Other performers often asked him for directions to a spot where they had to reach in time. Bhimanna would trot out all the minute particulars. 'If you follow this accurately, you will reach there a day in advance. Then sleep well, eat well, and sing well,' he would advise them.

He believed in what his father used to say: A Joshi home must be well stocked with food. When I went to Gadag to attend Grandfather Guracharya's last rites, I saw sacks upon sacks full of grains stocked in the house, more than enough to last three years. Every week Bhimanna got the petrol tank of his vehicle filled, just in case he had to start at an odd hour on a long journey.

Whether an audience consisted of fifty or five hundred members, Bhimanna would always pour his whole being into his singing. Sometimes there would be only a hundred listeners at a private concert, but Bhimanna would never sing mechanically. If the tanpuras were not correctly tuned, he would adjust them. And the audience would sit silently waiting for him. Half his success was thus earmarked by his bearing and these preliminaries. Everyone in the audience knew what was to follow would be a music banquet of note. The magic of his performances was a life-spanning and unfading joy for all. I have met many who had been enamoured by him from his very first performance. It opened for them a whole vista of happiness.

He was always patient and steady in initiating a raga. Then, ragas like Puriya, Yaman, Shuddh Kalyan would be lined up. Slowly the raga would unfold, grow, and finally speed up. By the time he touched the *shadja* (the basic note in Hindustani music or sa; meaning 'six notes are born' in Sanskrit), an hour was already over. The taans would shower like torrential rains, and a huge portrait of the raga would thus be painted. As a child I did not understand why he spent so much time before touching the next note. Why didn't he move on to the next one? However, as I grew up I began to see how our classical music and the ragas, along with the other arts, inherently shared borders with culture and spirituality. There is a time for every experience, every happiness to arrive. A hasty fulfilment can be incomplete. To the thirsty even ordinary water tastes sweet, and a delayed meeting with the loved one is all the more exciting. One cannot rush into youth and adulthood without childhood getting spoilt. That is how the patient unfolding of a raga has to be seen. Bhimanna, who knew this truth, adhered to it most devoutly. And after this elevating experience he would burst into an erotic Punjabi thumri, sending a shock of incredulity down the spine.

He would then choose a natya sangeet to be rendered for a full thirty minutes, for no one was in any hurry in those days. Following a cup of hot tea and a ball of tobacco would emerge Bhimanna's sonorous notes, binding the entire audience in a web. After listening to an elaborate exposition of the bada khayal of a raga, the audience would be all ears for Darbari, Malkauns,

Miya Malhar, Marwa, and Abhogi, if time permitted. The rendition would vibrate in memory long after it had ceased. The pleasure of such an experience beggars all description. The final Bhairavi would culminate in an entirely otherworldly experience for the listener. I sometimes used to feel that life after Bhimanna's Bhairavi was redundant. After one takes a dip into the Ganges, there is no need to come out again!

For a few days after such an unearthly experience I would be restless. I would repeat those notes and feel intoxicated if I could touch any of them in my singing. I never had the fortune to learn directly from Bhimanna; whatever crumbs I gathered were like those spilt when a sparrow feeds its young ones. This had unexpectedly good results, for I could reproduce some of his most complicated patterns. The sitar maestro Ustad Usman Khan once said to me, 'When we were learning, we used to be first introduced to the "face" of a raga in general; its grammar would follow in due course.' And here I was, having internalized Bhimanna's compositions so deeply that I could, as it were, hear them in my dreams too.

However, to learn his way was to sever oneself from the world of practical care, something that was beyond my control. Since he had taken another woman for a wife, Mother had reposed all her hopes in me, her only son then. Once my two sisters were married off, her well-being would entirely depend on my receiving a good education.

Once a young man from Dharwad came over to our place early in the morning. He spoke Kannada and wanted to learn from Bhimanna. We asked him if Bhimanna had agreed to teach him, for many aspirants arrived with a similar ambition. As it turned out, Bhimanna had indeed called him. But there was a problem; Bhimanna was away and not expected back in Poona for a week. We solved the young man's difficulty regarding accommodation by offering him a place to stay. He had brought his food with him, but Mother made him eat with us. Feeding an unexpected visitor was not a serious issue in those times.

The young man moved to the 'other' house after Bhimanna returned. I asked him not to mention his stay with us, otherwise he would be kicked out from there. Some good neighbours agreed to feed him in turns as long as he was taking lessons from Bhimanna. We, too, offered to feed him once a week. I also got a rent-free room for him at my friend Dilip Thatte's place. But he showed good form and Bhimanna allowed him to stay with them. He would occasionally describe the treatment that he was given there, including having to wash the family's clothes. He had no money, so I helped him occasionally. He would share his lessons with me and even taught me some ragas. I used to practise the famous composition of *'He Gokul gaon ka chora'* (O son from Gokul) set to raga Multani. My learning gradually came to an end as his visits became infrequent and I had to concentrate on my studies.

This student was Madhav Gudi, who became a noteworthy performer in due course. Ramakrishna Patwardhan and Narayan Deshpande, both from Bombay, were his seniors. Madhav Gudi did not have the guts to recognize me in 'her' presence. Shripati Padigar was also receiving training from Bhimanna at about the same time. Both of them were thoroughly devoted to him and spared no efforts in serving their guru. They opted to remain under his tutelage for a long time as Bhimanna showed no signs of stopping his performances even after turning seventy. As a result, these poor artists never grew to their full stature. Besides, they did not possess great depths of creativity and imagination, nor did they have their own separate identities and, thus, remained stunted. Shrikant

Deshpande, Sawai Gandharva's grandson, was Bhimanna's favourite and showed much promise as a vocalist, but, alas, he too had a short life.

∞

My college days went by fast, but I made many good friends during those years. Ashok Sahasrabuddhe, the topper, was one of them. His father C.G. Sahasrabuddhe was a noted scholar with an endless string of degrees suffixed to his name. I became close to this highly cultured family. It was a learning experience to be with them, not to forget the generous hospitality of my friend's mother. The jaggery-stuffed chapattis made by her with a big blob of pure ghee on them had no match. Ashok got admission into the prestigious Indian Institute of Management Calcutta, and became my source of news of Bhimanna's concerts in that city.

There would be five thousand present in the auditorium, while another ten thousand stood outside listening. Advance booking was the only way to get a ticket. Once I sent Bhimanna's handwritten note to Ashok, which gained him an easy entry into the auditorium. He told me that he saw a photograph of Bhimanna in a taxi. The passionate Bengalis were naturally enamoured by and engulfed in Bhimanna's soulful music.

I was shocked when I heard that Ashok was among the casualties in the 1976 Bombay–Madras aeroplane crash in Bombay. He had taken over as the GM of DelStar company after completing his MBA. Since then every aeroplane crash invariably reminds me of him.

I was in my BSc final in the year 1966. I did well in all papers except physics, which brought down my overall percentage.

A number of my friends took a break ('drop', as it was popularly known then) and did well in the finals. I could not afford to do so and hence joined a course in electronics at Wadia College. I was not much interested in studies. Meanwhile I landed a job in the Swastik Rubber Factory with the help of Ashok's brother-in-law, Mr Patwardhan. Good jobs were not easy to get in those days, but I never pressed Bhimanna to recommend me to anyone for a job. Eventually I got a good position in the defence production department of the central government in 1970. This opened a new chapter in my life as also in the life of my family.

A feeling of stability prevailed with the regular inflow of income from my job. Earlier we depended on Bhimanna's alms, often living on credit. I had hated it and got really fed up with the situation. But things changed now.

Talks about my marriage started at home, but for a long time I had been in love with Maya (Manjiri) Kulkarni, who was working temporarily as a school teacher after graduation. Although she had received her schooling in Poona, her college education was completed at Bijapur in Karnataka and she spoke Marathi, English, and Kannada quite comfortably.

My younger sister Usha now stood next in line and we started looking for a suitable match for her. She was fair and good-looking. We came upon a young man called Ravindra Kulkarni, an engineer who had a good job. He had no parents and his aunt had raised him. We spoke about it to Bhimanna, but 'she' refused to spend the customary money on the ceremonies. Finally the wedding was settled. I had to spend hours with Bhimanna, requesting him for the money needed for the customs. I married after a gap of fifteen days. 'She' was extremely close-fisted when it came to spending on us and had tried to persuade Bhimanna that my sisters should join a nursing course rather than do a college degree. Mother and I were adamant in that matter and did not allow 'her' evil plans to succeed.

Everybody in the Joshi clan, including my grandfather, attended Usha's marriage. But he could not make it to my marriage just fifteen days later as my stepuncle Damodar, too, was getting married. The other relatives camped in Poona for those fifteen days. My marriage with Maya Kulkarni created ripples in our circles, as love marriages were rare in those days. Her father Mr Shastri, who had become a Kulkarni through adoption, and her maternal uncle Yadwad were known to Bhimanna. Her uncles V.G. Shastri and A.G. Shastri were senior officers at the Central Bank and gave a very dignified reception to Bhimanna. 'She', too, attended the wedding and, along with Mother, was given due respect by the Shastris at a ceremonial banquet. 'She' was seated next to Mother at the ceremonial wedding lunch. 'She' had not been treated so respectfully even in her own son's marriage for he had gone to Alandi, a pilgrimage site near Poona and, after marrying secretly, had come to our house to seek the blessings of the 'elder mother'—my mother.

My honeymoon at the hill station of Mahabaleshwar was a modest affair as I had no cash to spare, since household demands drained most of my salary. Dr Kashinath Ghanekar, the veteran Marathi actor, was also staying at the same hotel, Bharat Hotel. He sat in the yard with a few friends, indulging in rather rowdy laughter with them. One of them felt a little embarrassed that their raucous talk might cause a nuisance to others, whereupon the actor said, 'In fact, it is a great enjoyment for them. They should pay us fees for it.' I shut the door of my room and started to sing the well-known bhajan *Teerth Vitthal, kshetra Vitthal* (Vitthal Himself is the holy water and place of pilgrimage) with great passion. When it was over, there was a knock on my door. On opening it I saw Dr Ghanekar standing in front of me. He asked me who I was. By this time his friends had gathered around. I introduced myself and asked them, 'Who should pay the fees now, and to whom?' Their laughter was my reward.

Soon after our wedding my wife got a permanent appointment in a school and our 'double' income started, bringing some financial stability to our home. I was now the master of the house and looked after all expenses, including whatever Mother needed. My uncle Narayankaka was working in the API Scooters Company. Bhimanna recommended for me a vehicle and a scooter was allotted to me from the special quota. My banker friend Suresh Deshpande sanctioned the required loan and I started enjoying riding my scooter; an old dream had finally come true! More than half a dozen persons stayed together in the two-room house, including two relatives from Mother's side who had got jobs in Poona.

We soon got set into a routine with our regular jobs, and the house hummed with activities every day. My wife took care of the kitchen after returning from her work in the evening. We ate together in a happy and healthy atmosphere. She was, indeed, an excellent cook. I had no regrets about love marriage as my wife looked after all of us efficiently and fed us well. Mother, too, had some mental peace now. One of our high-profile relatives had married a rich girl who had no kitchen skills and was therefore sent back to her maternal home to learn them. The old adage that the way to a man's heart is through his stomach seemed to be true, after all!

Post-dinner home chores kept my wife occupied till late in the evening. Rats had a field day on the tiled roof. Marital pleasures started late every night, which sometimes caused irritation to me. I began to feel that the situation had to change for the better. I had a choice of moving to government quarters through a transfer, which, however, meant leaving Mother and my young siblings to fend for themselves. Even so the desire for better living conditions was getting stronger with each passing day. I needed to put aside a part of our earnings to enjoy some comforts in the future. I felt that here lay the opportunity to take lessons in singing and, therefore, I started taking tuition from Prahladbuwa Joshi after returning from office. He did not charge me any fees as he wished to honour Bhimanna.

Prahladbuwa Joshi had served the nizam of Hyderabad from 1942 to 1944. Being a native of Kundgol—where his parents lived—he used to frequent the place. He was a good friend of Bhimanna. And when Bhimanna's guru, Sawai Gandharva Kundgolkar, unexpectedly ceased giving lessons to him—as a result of which he was in a state of depression—Prahladbuwa had taken him to Hyderabad to give him a change of scene.

Both of them stayed there for a few months in a bungalow allotted to him by the nizam. Soon Kumar Gandharva also joined them. Many tales of this merry company have been narrated to me by my guru. As Pralhadbuwa Joshi said:

We took turns to cook for ourselves. My duty was to sing to one of the sons of the nizam [Prince Muajjam] from 9:00 p.m. to 2:00 a.m. every day, as he suffered from insomnia. We used to buy more than ten litres of milk every day and boil it till it thickened. It was a rule that when we came together at night, we would drink a glass of milk and start our riyaz. This would continue as long as the milk lasted. Tired of cooking for ourselves once, we ate thirteen bhakris each at a mess. The next day, the keeper of the mess did not allow us to enter. But soon Bhimsen returned to his normal self and went back to Gadag.

I continued to take singing lessons for about eight months, but had to stop as I developed gastric troubles which, for a long time, could not be diagnosed. When I went to the teacher after office hours, I would be so hungry and weak that I had no control over my voice. Eventually, I had to undergo surgery for removal of my appendix, but nothing serious was diagnosed then either. As a result I continued to suffer for a whole year. It was the homeopath Dr Gurjar who cured me completely. I cannot forget his help.

Years after reading an English novel I understood why I had suffered from the ailment. My doctor had been prescribing Mexaform, the product of a multinational pharmaceutical company against which a Japanese doctor had initiated an inquiry. He fought a long battle and got the drug banned. During my hospitalization at the King Edward Memorial Hospital, Bhimanna came to see me along with 'her'. 'She' had brought half a dozen oranges that were given to me with studied indifference. 'She' never let him come alone, lest he get emotional and help us out with money. Being a government employee I was entitled to reimbursement of my medical expenses, but, even then, the expenses were difficult to meet with. I frequently had to take loans from my friends, which I returned later, but I never begged him for any help. I may sound detached now, but at that time it was always an excruciating experience for me.

During my stomach ailment one of my friends, Dr Bal Agashe, took me to a psychiatrist who said that my trouble could have roots in my mental agitation. Possibly, yes, because questions about self-identity and my distress over the way Bhimanna treated us was a painful source of our suffering. I never understood why he did not give me any training in singing although he knew that I had the talent. It tortured me to no end.

My firstborn came in a year's time in March 1971. I was at Bijapur from where I telephoned Bhimanna to break the news. His responded coldly, 'All right'. And he put down the receiver. It hurt me for a time, but I consoled myself with the thought that there must have been someone around and hence the coldness. Grandfather Guracharya, however, came for the naming ceremony. My mother-in-law sprinkled the customary gold flowers on my son as a blessing. The child was named Rahul and we were very happy.

Soon after this Usha, my younger sister, delivered a stillborn baby and I had to cremate it. I was unable to stop weeping the whole while. Usha took ill due to the bereavement. Even so Bhimanna did not come to console and comfort her, though, at about the same time—as reported by a teacher in my wife's school—he was seen carrying food for his sister-in-law who was also in labour.

I was highly perturbed and angered by Bhimanna's frigidity and indifference. I went to him in a rage and picked up a noisy quarrel with him. Do the great forget their basic humanity, after all? It is a pity that they have to live with a mask on their faces throughout. I had to borrow money from friends to meet with the expenses on these various matters. However, we got over this bitterness in due course. Whenever I attended his concerts thereafter, my mind, as it were, received showers of happiness that washed away all the toxic feelings. He, too, would cast a loving glance at me. At those times I would feel that a single shower of Bhimanna's melodious music was worth a hundred blows of his indifference. I could bear any pain and mental torture as long as the world could enjoy Bhimanna's music!

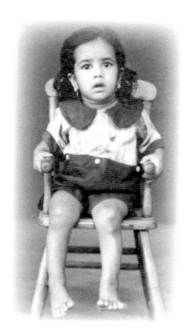

Raghu, 'Chip of the old block' in Guracharya's words, in 1947, Dharwad, Karnataka

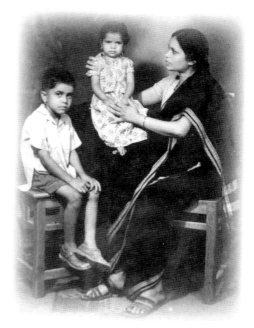

Sunanda with Raghavendra and Usha in 1950, Dharwad

Raghavendra's thread ceremony in 1955, Belgaum, Karnataka, seen here with his parents, Bhimsen and Sunanda

Raghavendra and Manjiri's wedding on 12 May 1970, Pune

Bhimsen and Sunanda at the thread ceremony of their grandsons, Rahul and Atul, with other family members on 17 May 1982, Pune

Raghavendra and Manjiri at the drilling rig in 1987, Pune

Raghavendra, Rahul, Bhimanna, and Atul in front of the first new car in 1989, Pune

Bhimanna with his grandsons, Atul and Rahul, in March 1989, Pune

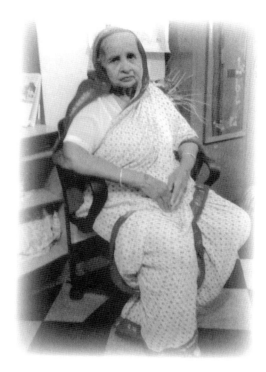

Bhimanna's second
mother Godabai in 2013,
Gadag, Karnataka

Bhimanna's father
Gururaj alias Guracharya
in 1979 Gadag

Raghavendra with his family on 5 November 2013, Pune

Four generations of the Joshi family in January 2003, Pune

Bhimsen Joshi, awarded the Bharat Ratna on 10 February 2009, Pune

Gangubai Hangal's letter consoling Raghavendra on his mother Sunanda's demise, 20 April 1992

Dr. Smt. Gangubai Hangal
DESHPANDE NAGAR, HUBLI - 580 029

Phone : 50152
65452
(Between 8 A.M & 9 P.M)
51736 66736
(Between 10 P.M. & 7 A.M)
D 20/4/92

Dear Raghavendra,
            my-self and all my family members felt very sorry to read in the members the sad demise of your mother. She was daring and humble lady. I felt sorry for not meeting her in recent years.
            Please accept my heartfelt condolences on death of your mother. All my family members have conveyed their condolences on death of your mother. It is really an irresparable loss. I pray God to give you all strength to bear this loss and also pray God to give peace to the departed soul.
                        Gangubai Hangal

Gadag. Shree   11-11-78

My dear Raghu,

I was very happy to receive your letter. I write to you in English because you will not follow if written in Kannada. I was so glad to hear that you were entering a new house owned by you that I felt quiet earnest to start for Pune. But my old age and weakness came in my way and I had to cancel most reluctantly coming to your place. I bless you all and hope that you may rise from strength to strength. I was very sorry that I could not do anything for you. Still you remember me in your happy moments, Chi—Bhima must have returned from America. He must be doing well even after this long journey and strenuous labour. Now my happiness

lies in seeing all happy in all respects. Remember me to your Mother with affection. Blessings to your brother and your wife and children.

Wish you all success in your frantic of new entrance in to the newly constructed building.

C.B. Joshi

Chi R. B. Joshi
269 Navi Peth
Pune

बुधवार!
हो सकता है
मलेरिया ही हो
क्लोरोक्विन गोली लें

15 भारत
INDIA

पिन PIN

Guracharya's letter to his grandson Raghavendra, 11 November 1978

Seven

BHIMANNA'S NEW FLAT in Rambaug Colony had a balcony facing the main street. Whenever passers-by saw him standing there, they would wave at him respectfully. The press always carried detailed descriptions of his performances. By now he was quite a well-known celebrity. In fact, Maharashtra was known to the rest of India for two personalities: Yashwantrao Chavan, the then chief minister of the state, and Bhimanna. He was honoured with the Padma Shree in 1972. He gave me a copy of the photograph of President V.V. Giri awarding him with the award.

One evening Madhukaka, then a pilot in the Indian Air Force, and his Punjabi wife knocked at our door. He would usually stay with Bhimanna, bringing excellent-quality fruits and Basmati rice for him. However, it happened once that he was received with a cold response and was, in fact, no longer a welcome guest with the 'other' family. He mentioned this to Mother with tears in his eyes. 'She' was always quick to get rid of relatives who tried to get close to Bhimanna. We were happy to welcome the couple and enjoyed a hot meal with them. Now the real problem was one of space in our two-room flat. Where would we accommodate the guests? Luckily my wife's maternal uncle Gajabhau Yadwad was visiting us then. He had a vacant three-room flat in the same building. The problem was solved. Such embarrassments were common for us in those days; our resources were meagre and the house was small, but we were happy. Mother always kept the house clean and tidy. However, during the annual Sawai Gandharva Sangeet Mahotsav, it was a difficult time as visitors thronged our place and the bitter cold of December in Poona was unbearable, for there was a shortage of warm clothing.

There was never a fixed time for Bhimanna to knock at our door. Once he returned from a concert in Jalandhar and reached Poona in the dead of night. We heard a knock at our door, followed by 'Nandi, I'm here. Open the door!' I opened the door immediately. He entered with a gorgeous bouquet, which he placed in my hands. The gentle whiff of a perfume also entered with him. He asked for curd-rice, which my wife prepared with a liberal tadka on it, the way he liked it. I made his bed in the other room, and Mother and he slept there.

In the wee hours came another loud knock. We wondered who it could be at such an odd hour. On opening the door, we found 'her' standing there with her people and a couple of male servants. 'Is this a place to live in? How dirty everything is!' she shouted. Bhimanna came out and was dragged away. My wife was furious at this effrontery and shouted, 'If you behave this way again, I will break your leg!' 'She' was taken aback and said to Bhimanna, 'See how your daughter-in-law insults me!' When the invading party had moved away a little, Bhimanna turned back and said to my wife in Kannada, 'Good job!' The woman was vocal with her complaints, 'I suffer so much!' I retorted, 'The bulk does not show it'.

It was 'she' who had put everyone in such an impossible position, but her hypocrisy knew no bounds. We were relieved to note that while this vulgar show was taking place no neighbour of ours showed any impolite curiosity about it. They were decent people, indeed. One of them, Sudhatai Gadgil, however, overheard the whole episode and felt great sympathy for us.

Altercations became frequent as time went by and 'she' snatched every chance to tarnish my image in Bhimanna's mind. After a while he started bringing the monthly cash himself to Mother; sometimes he would send it through a trusted person, or he would leave it with our neighbours, the Gadgils. Meanwhile I had set up my own house at Dhayari near Poona. The duty of picking up the monthly money now fell on my brother Anand and for him, too, it was a painful experience. Bhimanna continued to make the payment—just sufficient for Mother and Anand to meet with their household expenses, her medicines, and his tuition fees—as long as Mother lived.

Even so he would come to meet Mother in the small flat whenever he felt like it. After all, she was his legally wedded wife and society has no objection to such meetings.

My sister Sumangala was working as a school teacher and was now of a marriageable age. In 1973 we got her married to Mohan Raydurg, a young man from Dharwad. They settled down in their own house in a small village called Jambhulpada in Konkan, and worked hard as teachers. Their children, too, did well in life. Eventually we three siblings were married and settled, setting Bhimanna free of all responsibilities. Anand was eighteen years my junior; he completed his BSc and married late.

Bhimana's children from 'her' did not have a smooth sailing. Money alone could not impress seekers of marital alliances.

As Madhukaka died prematurely I got his son Dhruv married to Sucheta, the daughter of my wife's friend Polas. Bhimanna came to bless the couple and complimented me.

We had a second son, Atul, and in due course we performed a joint thread ceremony for both my sons. Bhimanna and all our relatives attended the celebrations. The hall where the ceremony took place was well known for the good food it served. Bhimanna immensely enjoyed the vegetable pulao, and the caterers were grateful and pleased.

All the aunts were present in my small home and Shamakka (Mother's elder sister Shamala) ensured a steady flow of water supply from the handpump. Her place, Gadag, suffered from acute water shortage and Poona's sweet and ample water simply delighted her. She enjoyed the *gajar halwa* (a sweet dish made from carrots) prepared by my wife, something she had never eaten before. There was no end to the chats as old memories welled up among the family members. Bhimanna, too, was happy to meet all of them after several years. He called out to my aunt, 'Hi, Shamay!' And she replied fittingly, 'How are you, Bhimu?' The great Bhimsen of the world was only their very own Bhimu! It turned out to be a festival of love, affection, and memories. Bhimanna was a loving soul.

I used to invite Grandfather Guracharya to all religious ceremonies held at my place. If he could not make it he would write letters and shower blessings and good wishes, two of which I still possess. In one of them he says, 'Raghu dear, you have been a loving grandson to invite me every time for ceremonies. I feel very happy. I know that I could do little to help you in life. I am sad about it. Be sure that my blessings will always protect you.' I belong to a tradition where blessings carry immense value and, therefore, I have still kept those letters. I always bowed before Bhimanna only for his blessings which, I have no doubt, led me through life and brought me happiness.

∞◦∞

One of Bhimanna's accompanists told me an interesting story. Once the entire party was travelling by car to Dharwad for a performance and they were running late. He was in a depressed mood, harried by unending family bickering. The car crossed through Belgaum city. Then someone suggested to him, 'It's already eleven o'clock. The audience must have dispersed. Let's go back to Poona now.' 'Don't worry about it,' he said. 'They love me. Give me just half an hour more.' The car reached M.K. Hubli, about thirty kilometres before Belgaum, and they halted near the temple of Narasimha, our family deity. It was winter and bitterly cold. Bhimanna entered the nearby river and stood neck-deep in the water for twenty minutes. After chanting the *Mangalarati*, he got into the car, asked the driver who had been hired for the trip to take the back seat, drove the car, and they reached Dharwad within an hour. People were still waiting patiently at the auditorium and, as the car entered through the gates, a wave of cheers went up. Bhimanna kept the audience entranced till four in the morning. Lucky are those who listened to the unearthly performance that night!

Once on the eve of the Sawai Gandharva Sangeet Mahotsav, he lost his temper and drove off by himself in his car for Hubli. On the way he halted at Mahabaleshwar where he met a friend and had dinner at Sahasrabuddhe's Hotel Girivihar. He asked Dada Sahasrabuddhe whether he could have bhakri to eat. 'Anything for you,' replied Dada and invited Bhimanna to stay overnight and leave in the morning. However, Bhimanna proceeded to Satara.

He bought petrol near Nipani. A dispute arose over the payment, as the pump operator had tried to swindle Bhimanna who was slightly tipsy. He left the car there and took a lift in a truck to Nipani, where he made a phone call to his friend Sarekoppa Bangarappa, the then chief minister of Karnataka.

A police jeep and an Ambassador car arrived and he proceeded to Gangubai Hangal's place in Hubli. The next day his car, which he had left at the petrol pump, was delivered to him with the tank filled up. Obviously the police had twisted the petrol-pump man's arm! Back home in Poona, the news broke that Bhimanna had gone missing.

By now Bhimanna had started performing abroad as well. He brought a nylon sari for Mother and a small pack of almonds for us from America. At the customs check, Bhimanna had to pay duty for excess items. Thereafter, we stopped getting to know about his foreign visits. His LP records were being sold like hot cakes.

Prabhakar Rao, who had arranged Bhimanna's programmes during his visit to America, told me later that whenever he was by himself Bhimanna spoke affectionately only about me. I was overjoyed to hear it.

Once when I was looking for one of his LPs, Bhimanna gave me a letter of introduction to The Gramophone Company (HMV) at Bombay and asked his student Narayan Deshpande to accompany me. I was given a record player and some records by the company, which was a pleasant surprise for me.

Bhimanna's other house was now overflowing with the products of his earnings. He wished to build a bungalow in the Rajendranagar area of Poona, for which a contract was given to Vajram, the son-in-law of the poet B.B. Borkar. My mother broached the need to have a house of her own and Bhimanna said he would try to give the money. He gave us an excuse that he was under the pressure of expenses on the bungalow under construction, but he was spending lavishly on the new house and furniture. I was amused to note how company affects a man—Bhimanna had learnt the art of telling lies from his alliance. I felt sorry for him.

After a few years he did give some money to Mother, however, by then I had already built a bungalow through a bank loan and the money we had saved in Dhayari in 1976. Even so, in his biography of Bhimanna, Nadkarni has written erroneously that Bhimanna gave me money to build my bungalow. I do not know whether I should laugh or be angry that he had not taken the trouble to find out the truth, which was that the money given to Mother had been deposited by her in a bank just in case she should need it in future. That was the first and last time Bhimanna gave her a good sum of money in a single instalment. By this time Bhimanna was a millionaire, but he possessed nothing of his own.

News from the 'other' house flowed in occasionally. The elder son had knocked down an old man with his motorbike, and had been dragged into a lawsuit. Bhimanna's advocate Kelkar told me once that Bhimanna was much perturbed during those days. 'I don't know where my money goes. I cannot pay your mother,' he would keep repeating to me. I would then retort, 'Yes, the king of concerts has to keep up a show, after all!' He understood what I meant, but he had been stripped down to the bare essentials. I did not want to embarrass him anymore.

At the same time, Bhimanna had sent his elder son to the USA for higher studies, but the hero returned without any achievements.

When I started constructing my house in Dhayari, the water was initially supplied by a neighbour, the reputed writer Pandit Mahadevshastri Joshi. However, soon after the water level of his well started dropping. I tried to engage a local water supplier, but the supply was scanty. The construction work was nearing completion, but water shortage posed a problem. Then, most unexpectedly, unseasonal rains lashed the village and a deep ditch in our compound was filled with rainwater to the brim. This was almost a miracle—as good as the one in *The Ten Commandments* when Moses parts the waters of the Red Sea to help his people escape from the Egyptian army. It helped me complete the construction of my house.

I painted the house myself and got the electric fittings fixed. My brother Anand helped me. The work would start in the morning when we carried the lunchbox from our house in Poona and returned home only by the evening, by which time we would be exhausted. The main problem, however, was the lack of regular water supply. The promoter had absconded without completing the work on the approach roads and the side drainages. Eventually, I called a meeting of all the plot-holders, many of whom were from Bombay. We got the plots demarcated clearly. My neighbour Paranjape and I completed the approach road. I also got a bridge built over the road and looked after the vacant plots for many years to come. I undertook the planting of trees along the roadside. It was a tough time as I had to run between my home and the new site. But the greenery pleased my eyes and, what is more, Mother spent her last few years in my house in peace and comfort.

The water supply, however, remained an acute problem. I purchased tools like crowbar and spade, and started to dig a well in one corner of the plot. For about four months, on every holiday, I would come all the way from Poona to work on the plot. While I continued to sweat it out, a little earthen pitcher was my only source of water. It was a back-breaking job for sure.

The soil began to show traces of moisture when I reached down to a depth of twelve feet. But, another three feet down, solid granite blocked the crowbar. Since modern implements like stone breaker and jackhammer were not in regular use, I bought some mining powder from the market, stuffed it into small pieces of an old rubber tube from a bicycle, and fixed a long wick. However, the explosions turned out to be so powerful that pieces of rock were hurled into the sky, many of which landed on the asbestos roof of my house and broke it. I had to stop the experiment. The only benefit was the knowledge of using a crowbar and a spade!

In the meantime, I took up the study of groundwater and methods of exploring it. The British Council Library had a good stock of books on the subject. Being an employee of the defence department I also had access to military manuals. The Germans had developed a technique for digging borewells, using water-exploring instruments like magnetometers and resistivity gadgets. I consulted a geologist in Poona who ruled out all possibility of water on my plot. Close by stood the Marina Poultry Farm, which depended on tankers for receiving water since the same geologist had given a negative report to them ten years ago.

At this time I got to know about a water diviner, Hughes Davenport, in Poona. With the help of Mr Mhatre, a drilling expert, I got Davenport to come to my plot. My neighbours, Appa Supnekar and Appa Paranjpe, had also built small bungalows by now. Davenport walked over the three plots and identified certain spots for digging.

Finally a spot where only a handpump could operate was identified. The work of digging a borewell with a diesel engine went on for a month. Two workers laboured on it; I would give them a hand at times. Since I have a flair for using gadgets and machines, I began to understand the entire process. One day the workers announced that the water source had been located sixty feet underground. After installing a handpump, the supply started intermittently, ten buckets at a time after a gap of ten minutes. In those days Dhayari, although on a higher level, suffered from acute water shortage although Sinhgad road had ample water from a canal connected to a dam. Neighbours started making a beeline for my water tap; there were people coming from the Benkar area, Kaluram Pokle from the hillside, and the Thopte family, all about a kilometre away from our place. Thopte saw an opportunity in this newfound source: he increased the rent of his clients. If a client asked about the availability of water, Thopte would point to our handpump!

I invited Davenport to locate the presence of water on the other plots also. He had noted my interest and involvement in finding water; so one day he placed the divining rod in my hand and said, 'You try'. As I began to walk over the area which he had marked, the rod bent down. Indeed, the two words 'You try' became the rallying cry for me and changed the course of my life. My mind started registering clearly whether water sources lay in a spot as I walked over it with the divining rod in my hand. Pretty soon I could spot with good precision where a stream was flowing underground. The revelation opened a way for me to help people around me.

Much advanced research has been done in Russia about water divining. Such diviners enter the alpha state of mind, which is akin to trance. A distant relative, Padma Bhushan Dr Sheshagiri, explained the mystery to me. He told me that even an ordinary brain has far greater capacities than a supercomputer. I honed my skills in collaboration with Mr Davenport.

My work in Dhayari started when I successfully identified several spots for neighbours where water was available.

In those days it lay on the outskirts of Poona. Bungalows and housing societies were coming up everywhere, but water supply continued to be a severe problem. Tap water was still not available. I identified a borewell spot for common water supply on Mr Laygude's plot where we found a forceful, strong supply of water. Neighbours like Laygude, Kamble, A.H. Joshi, a chartered accountant, formed a society, built a common water supply tank, and arranged to fill it with water regularly from the borewell. It worked successfully for fifteen years, until Dhayari was included in Poona Corporation, which took over water management in due course.

My divining assignments started regularly. I used to visit Karad every Saturday and stay with my friend Kulkarni, who looked after me with great care. The following morning I would visit the surrounding farms and locate water for the farmers there. I successfully identified several spots and the problem was eased for many of them.

A certain Mr Bhosale had purchased a thirty-five-acre plot at Bahe near Islampur. He got it at a low price as chances of striking water were dim. I walked over the plot and identified a spot where, after digging a dug well, water was found twenty feet below the ground. A pump was fitted and a bountiful supply began. He went down another thirty-five feet where even more forceful streams were found. In a short time he became the owner of a richly fertile farm. He celebrated the success and threw a lavish feast at which I was the guest of honour.

I continued to attend Bhimanna's concerts and meet him after the performances. We were still living in Poona as I had not been allotted an electricity connection despite several applications. One day Bhimanna took Mother to Dhayari along with his tabla accompanist Gulam Rasool. I joined them after my office hours. Bhimanna was playing with a pair of huge Labrador dogs, which were a terror in the area. Bhimanna said, 'The dog that will bark at me is yet to be born!' Possibly dogs, too, could sense the subtle music in him.

Gulam Rasool was observing *roza* (religious fasting) and ate nothing throughout the day. Bhimanna conversed in chaste Urdu with him. He was a very good ghazal singer and sang for us. It was a candlelight performance since we did not have any electricity. The next morning, after washing himself, Bhimanna needed hair oil. Since we were not living in the house, such small items were not kept there. He asked Mother for some cooking oil and applied it on his head! He knew how to make do with available resources.

Later that morning an electricity board vehicle stopped in front of my house and the connection was fitted within half an hour. Clearly enough, Bhimanna had pulled strings (and ears) somewhere. His recommendations gave several people good jobs too.

✥

I remember many of my experiences during my wanderings in search of water. On a hot, blazing day, with my friend Balasaheb Atkekar, I was visiting a village near Sangli, where a well was to be dug. Our throats were parched and the hot, dry dust flying up from under our feet was another challenge. On the steep slope of the land, we came upon a hut where a man gave us a jug of drinking water. The poor soul said, 'Sir, my well too is dry. Can you kindly help me?' Immediately

I took out my divining rod and started walking over his land. I sensed a water stream close to the well which was dry as the blasting had been badly done. I advised him to blast the boulder blocking the stream, and we moved on.

After a month or so, when I was going along the same route with the contractor, the man from the hut came running to me. He touched my feet and began to cry. Then he took us to the well. He had blasted the boulder and the well was filled with fresh water even during the hot summer. He told us why he was crying. His forefathers had died without getting water even after the well had been dug. They could have lived comfortably if they had had water. Some people are close to happiness, but happiness eludes these unfortunate ones.

Once I had to visit Miraj at the request of the Thorat family there. I was supposed to go to a village called Mangsuli near Miraj. The train reached four hours late, but my client was waiting for me at the station. After a cup of tea we began the survey that went on till noon when we took a lunch break. He came from a royal family and the food was lavish and rich. I continued to scout the whole area till evening, identified a few spots, and returned to Poona the next morning. After a month or so I got a letter telling me that the new well was full of water. It further said, 'You have opened the gates of heaven for me. Thank you.'

I can recall some strange situations as well. The place was a small village near Kolhapur. The man seeking my advice was a lecturer. I searched for water sources till noon on his land and identified some spots. Then we returned to his house where I was served a delicious lunch of bhakris and vegetables. Everything was so carefully cooked and delicious as if a raga delivered in the most chaste style of singing. In the afternoon the same exercise was continued on another plot.

This time a man carrying a sharp axe escorted me. I came to know later that the land was under violent dispute and attacks were feared!

At another place, after a lot of walking and hard work, we came to a small hut hoping to get some food. The poor man served us only water with jaggery added to it. That was all, but I liked the taste. I took a token fee of ten rupees and returned to Poona in a happy mood by a private truck. Indeed the work, although it was often tiring, gave me some of the happiest times of my life.

My services were in good demand and so I made a detailed study of the science of digging borewells. With a substantial loan facility from the Central Bank, I purchased the necessary equipment and a truck in Hyderabad. I resigned in 1985 and launched a small-scale company, Joshi Borewells.

The first borewell was dug on Bandukaka's plot in Secunderabad. It supplied ample water which helped him construct his bungalow. My wife was uneasy about my decision to resign my job as I had been recently promoted. But her school job was secure. We had recently toured Kashmir, and Hotel Khayyam in Srinagar had charged only 310 rupees for four days! We were financially comfortable and we were happy.

Despite my growing assignments I saw Bhimanna regularly. He used to listen to the records of the performers of other gharanas (schools). He was particularly interested in Kumar Gandharva. And, of course, Abdul Karim Khan Sahib and Bal Gandharva were always his first choice during his solitary hours.

Eight

WHEN I DECIDED TO RESIGN my job, the fifteen years from 1970 that I had spent in the Chief Inspectorate of Armaments flashed through my mind. It had been a stable and well-paid central government job promising a good future. There was a well-disciplined atmosphere. In the office the foreman Mr Kohen, a Parsi gentleman, had initiated me into my work. Mr Yeolekar and Mr Phatak were my bosses. The other employees were from different regions and spoke different languages and it was a good learning experience in diversity. The other bosses like Colonel Iyengar and Mr Muttuswamy were strict disciplinarians at work, but friendly when we met in the dining room while sharing our lunch. A short post-lunch power nap and work would be taken up again.

We were young and enthusiastic about everything, including spirited discussions on politics, in-house backbiting, and other matters. My supervisor Mr Swaminathan, a Keralite, always got into heated discussions with me on the virtues of Carnatic as compared with Hindustani style of classical music. A peace treaty was finally entered into with the help of my friend Kanta Kulkarni over a hot plate of onion bhaji and tea in the office canteen.

For a few months we were full of love for Shivaji Maharaj. We studied closely the forts of Maharashtra. Then Mainkar, Dandekar, R.R. Bhide, Apte, and I formed a group. My hiking outfit resembled that of a soldier on duty, with a haversack, hunter shoes, knives, a flashlight, and other necessities. Jayant Badve lent me his Diana gun and bullets, and also instructed me in shooting rabbits and skinning them (until then I knew nothing about cutting open a creature). Finally we set out on our trek to Rajgad with loud slogans of 'Har har Mahadev!' We started climbing the mountain through the secret passage of the fort. It was such an exhausting exercise that we lay flat on the ground for quite a while on our way up. We realized for the first time that even one's own body is a weighty thing!

However, undaunted, we struggled and reached the top. While we were congratulating ourselves on our feat, we saw a pregnant woman carrying a heavy bundle of firewood on her head and climbing up the same route! The sight deflated our self-esteem. We rested in the temple of Goddess Bhavani up there, drank the clean, cold water from the tank, and were greatly refreshed. All around us lay the awesome and exhilarating beauty of untamed nature and my mind was filled with joy. The entire mountain was covered with golden and purple flowers. A bonus treat was the presence of the writer and historian G.N. Dandekar, who also happened to be there. He brought to life the full history of Rajgad for us. Then we returned to the temple.

We had carried our lunch, but for dinner we built a small fire. I prepared khichri with rice and lentils and spices which had been packed by my wife. I liberally poured pure ghee on it, fried papads, and we polished off everything as we were famished by the exercise—both climbing and culinary. By then it was late evening. We took some painkillers and slept like logs.

The next day we trekked from Rajgad to Torna fort. A guide showed us the way. By evening it started to rain. Suddenly, we saw cattle bounding towards us from the hilltop. Apte slid down the hillside a couple of times, broke into tears, and started cursing us for making him join the trek. Some of us were quite energetic, but no one volunteered to help him. I felt sorry for him and carried him on my back. The guide kept encouraging us with his 'just a few steps more' mantra. Fatigued and hungry, we reached a place called Velha. I put Apte down, took off my shirt, and discovered that my shoulder was bleeding. 'Bravo, bloke!' said Mainkar, and from that day on I came to be addressed as 'Bloke'.

After that I organized several such treks. During one such trek I was on the verge of slipping down into a deep valley, but I stopped the downward slide by planting my shoes firmly into the earth. I was saved. Looking back on all those feats, one tends to feel quite amused. I would advise political parties bearing Shivaji's name to select their recruits by putting them through the test of entering the Rajgad fort by the secret entrance.

Through these activities, I came across a number of interesting people—the talented and the crackpots, the hard-working, the shirkers, and the sycophants—and made many trusted and good friends. In winters we used to enjoy eating bread and boiled eggs in a hot and spice gravy in the inner room of the Proof Range (Firing Range where all newly manufactured ammunition is tested by firing it using the respective weapons) of the factory. It would transport us to heaven then. Ulhas, Ashok Gadgil, and Bhide were my companions during these eating bouts.

I met the future eminent cartoonist Mangesh Tendulkar during those days. When I told him that I was Bhimsen Joshi's son he quipped, 'Then you are in the wrong place here'. He was equally good at painting pictures with words. Hulsure, one of my friends, sent to the prime minister an elaborate plan for connecting the major rivers of India as a solution to its chronic water problem. Another friend, Kripashankar Sharma, was an ardent Dilip Kumar fan.

Within the factory all the rules and regulations laid out by the British were followed meticulously. This distinction between 'civil' and 'military' exists even today.

Side by side with honest and straightforward officers we also saw corrupt and dishonest men. We saw malingerers during the war. The entire office was, as it were, a cross section of our nation. The reservation rule had killed all prospects of upward mobility. No one could be removed from service. As a result, many sweepers and lower ranks became adept in shunning work and shirking duty. However, one sweeper from Lucknow was a model of conscientiousness. He spoke chaste Urdu and entertained us with many *shayari*s (stanzas of Urdu poetry) and ghazals at our request. Some small traders had also come up in the office, selling bhel, sweets, garments, and the like. A Sindhi storekeeper was a secret moneylender from whom the brigadier, too, borrowed money sometimes. Some *varkari*s (pilgrims) who were totally devoted to God Vithu were also employed there and worked quite well.

In the compound there was a hut with a tin roof which roasted everything under it during summer, and the paan vendor Kutti suffered badly. On one of my rounds I saw a flowering tree. I cut off two branches, planted them, one on each side of Kutti's hut, and advised him to water them every day. Within a few months, they started to grow and, in the course of time, even covered the roof and brought some relief to him. Kutti started a regular supply of paan and *elaichi* (cardamom) to me as quid pro quo!

The memory of two incidents during those days has remain with me even today. I was on escort duty with some equipment that I had to carry on the train on which I was travelling. The train was late, and I was waiting on the deserted platform. At that moment Secunderabad Express pulled in, but started to move on without halting. Suddenly, I heard someone shouting, '*Admi gir gaya!*' (A man has fallen under the train!) It was a soldier who had been trying to take his luggage off the moving train. I rushed towards the engine and gesticulated to the driver to stop. Eventually the train came to a halt, but I did not want to see what had happened to the man, for I was sure that he had been cut to pieces. A crowd gathered around the spot and somebody shouted, '*Bach gaya!*' (He has been saved). He was badly bruised and in a swoon. I recalled the saying 'Nothing can kill one whom the gods wish to save'. I was very happy that, in a way, I had been instrumental in saving his life.

I was a new recruit in the office basketball team, but had learnt to play well within a short time. We were divided into two teams, A and B, and I captained the B team. Thomas, a national-level athlete was on my team, while the other team comprised sweepers and workers. In the tournament, after playing with other office teams and beating them, both the teams reached the semi-final. My team was now pitted against another team under an officer.

The match began and we quickly realized that we were no match for the rival team; they were far superior. Even so, in the second half, we gave a neck-to-neck fight and were close in scores. I was in a fighting spirit and went forward with the ball, looked at the ring, and hurled the ball. It was a clean slide through the basket. We had won amid thunderous cheers. I dropped two more clean 'baskets' amid sky-rending claps. I became a hero in the office.

The next day while we were practising on the grounds and I showed good form, the captain of the other team remained tongue-tied and did not cheer for me. Thomas was irritated and said, 'You cannot do in your whole life what our Joshi did in yesterday's game!' The colour drained from the captain's face. A number of spectators told me that my performance the previous day was world-class. However, the captain of the opponent team 'fixed' the next match and we lost. I knew why he was jealous of me; he was a tabla player of sorts and was in the inner circle of a singer who was always compared to Bhimanna. He was one of those whom the bug of self-love had bitten. I pity such poor fellows who never understand the divine touch of music and remain petty-minded all their lives!

I kept learning and participated in many extended study programmes like basic armament, basic explosives, advanced small arms course, and so on, with the intention of getting opportunities to tour the country and seeing new places and other important armament factories. I went to Ishapor to visit the rifle factory along with many Bengali friends. One day after the lectures were over, we went to the canteen where a sizable crowd had assembled. Someone whispered in my ears that they had come to meet me as they had been told that I was Bhimsen Joshi's son. There were more than a hundred and they requested me with folded hands to convey their regards to Bhimsenji! I was moved to see how well-loved Bhimanna was everywhere.

I had to resign in a hurry as I had to go to Hyderabad to get a truck cabin. My boss, Mr Bodas, knew me well and he released me without delay. There was no time even to accept a formal send-off.

I got the drilling ring and began work in Dhayari. I dug borewells for Sarpanch Ranoji Pokle, Chavan-Patil, and other small farmers around. They would feel relieved when they first saw the water gushing out ceaselessly. This was a water revolution in Dhayari. I expanded my work to suburban Poona as well. I located good sources of water where geophysical experts had given negative reports. This helped build my reputation far and wide.

Meanwhile I had been to Bijapur in order to meet my mother-in-law Champakka, who was not keeping well. My reputation as a diviner had travelled ahead of me there. One day Riyaj Faruki, the liaison officer of Al-Ameen Charitable Fund Trust, came to consult me. His trust had purchased 125 acres of land at Torvi in order to build a medical college and a hospital. Geophysical experts from Chandigarh had not given a positive report. We went there by car. It was a vast stretch of land, which was spread over many places, and I would need a couple of days to confirm. After ten days I visited the place again and identified ten spots where water sources were sure to be found. I was asked to submit a quotation of estimated costs for the work, which I mailed from Poona. I received a cheque of a small amount as an advance towards my fees. Thereafter, I went to Bijapur for the work.

It was an unusually hot summer day and the Karnataka government had declared drought officially in the state. I stood in one spot with my truck, assembled the rig, cracked open a coconut to propitiate the gods, and started the drilling work. As dust began to whirl out, a crowd collected. The people spoke in Kannada and were making fun of the whole exercise. They were saying that not a drop would be available at such a height since there wasn't any even at lower levels around, and that it would be a waste of labour because drilling borewells had been tried twenty times, and so on and so forth. They did not know that I knew Kannada well.

Almost four hours of drilling had been carried out. There was not even a stunted bush for shade. The entire area echoed with the loud noise of the compressor. Suddenly I noticed that dust clouds were receding. I pushed forward at the positive signs. Five feet more of drilling and drops of water started spouting up. At the next thrust there was a powerful spurt, followed by gushing water. The bystanders began to shout out in surprise. It was then that I spoke to them in Kannada. The workers directed the flow into a channel down the dry stream. The powerful current gushed on and on. Faruki and his advocate Jahagirdar came running. They stood wonderstruck. I had dug down hardly 160 feet.

I took nine more bores and all of them supplied different quantities of water current. Four of them turned out to be profuse in supply. In due course, a big medical college and a hospital were constructed. The news went around Bijapur like wildfire and I could not go back to Poona for the next six months as assignments and contracts would not stop coming in. Some newspapers also highlighted the event.

I dug borewells in places like Babanagar and Bijjargi in Bijapur district; this district is famous for its grape cultivation, giving stiff competition to Tasgaon in Maharashtra. Clients began to queue up for their turn. I still remember a farmer whom I had helped. The water levels were rather low in Karnataka and farmers had to dig the earth fairly deep for water. One evening I reached a property along with Mr Denganwaru, an employee of the state transport department. Wells had been sunk with bore work, but without good results. However, they had not tried one well that stood at a higher level on the border of the farm. I examined the well and identified a particular spot. Since it was late in the evening, we ended the day with a good dinner with the farmers, after which I went to sleep. The work would begin the next day.

As planned the drilling began in the morning. Water began to well up just twenty-five feet below the well's bottom level. A water pump was fitted and within a short time the entire farm was watered. We went down a hundred feet. The farmer was so overjoyed that he arranged a special treat of *sewai kheer* for me. When it was time for me to say goodbye, he began to weep. 'Sahib,' he said, 'we have not slept for the last six months. I had to move my cattle to my relatives in Sangli. I will sleep like a log tonight.'

My visits to different places acquainted me with the realities of life, one of them being the importance of having money. I had once been denied entry to Bhimanna's concert because I did not have money to buy a ticket. I was convinced that I had to make all possible efforts to survive with dignity in this world. Bhimanna was worried when I told him that I was resigning in order to launch my own borewell enterprise. '*Oho*, planning to become rich overnight?' he asked. 'The others are living like parasites on someone else's wealth. You want me to stay put where I am,' I retorted. He understood and seemed to be pleased. I had to forego all employment benefits as I had not completed the designated service period.

I immersed myself completely in work. Despite an initial rough patch, within a couple of years, I established my credentials in Maharashtra and Karnataka. I used to flash my income tax documents before Bhimanna. Then I decided to buy a car and requested him to accompany me, else I would not buy it. He agreed.

We got a brand new Fiat car from Ram Agency, which was owned by Bhimanna's friend. Bhimanna put his hand lovingly around my son's shoulders when we photographed ourselves there. Then he drove us all the way to his bungalow. He was overjoyed that I had bought a new car with my own money. Then he turned to the front door of his bungalow and said loudly, 'At least come out to see what he has achieved'. 'She' and her retinue poured out and stood around the car. 'She' noticed that the rear seat was piled high with boxes of sweets. 'Looks like quantities of sweets have been purchased.' 'Of course! When I have spent so much on a new car, why should I be close-fisted when buying sweets? Here is a box for you too,' I said proudly and placed a box in 'her' hands. The next day my brother Anand got married. Bhimanna spent the entire day with Mother and we drove the new couple home in our new car. Bhimanna presented me with four books on car mechanics.

When I went to visit a family friend, Gore Aunty, I was taken aback when she told me that 'she' was spreading a rumour that it was Bhimanna who had given me the new car as a present. Gore Aunty had refused to believe it for she knew the truth and she said so to those who were spreading the news. It was the Bank of Maharashtra that had sanctioned me a good loan for the car.

Once I had to do drilling at Dr Sangamnerkar's brother's bungalow close to Bhimanna's house. I requested him to come see how the work was done. Dr Sangamnerkar was very happy to have Bhimanna and invited him in for a cup of tea. I also drilled a well on the eminent writer Pandit Mahadevshastri Joshi's plot at Dhayari and the resultant good water supply helped irrigate his farm for many years to come. I was earning well and I repaid my bank loan well before time. I was their first client who was so particular about repaying loans.

Once when I was drilling at a place called Kesnand in Poona district I suddenly felt my hands stiffen as I was trying to climb out a well using a rope. I had been running a temperature a couple of days earlier and was weak. My hands were cramped.

Below me lay scattered our steel and iron implements. If I fell my body would be cut into shreds. I can never forget that crucial moment in my life: images of my wife, my children, my home, all flashed before my mind. I decided to slide down carefully and reached the bed, trembling violently with fear. My toes were hurt, but I was safe. Surely God and my good deeds had saved me. I had to be pulled up with a crane.

I got assignments in Poona too. One day I got a call for a survey and a car was arranged for me. I was taken to the bungalow of the eminent industrialist Neelkanth Kalyani. I selected two spots on his and his son's plot. In a couple of days I got a phone call informing me that water had been found just thirty feet below the ground. 'The sahib himself danced in the fountain for some time,' said the caller who turned out to be the eminent geophysicist Dr Budhajirao Mulik. 'You are an expert water diviner,' he complimented me. He also told me that there was no such thing as a water-exploring machine anywhere in the world. Nine borewells had been dug on Mr Kalyani's plot earlier but without success. Dr Mulik said, 'Anyone who can source water precisely in Maharashtra stands an excellent chance to become its chief minister!'

I had many assignments from Kalyani Industries in times to come. At Mahabaleshwar, the spot I had identified had water level just 120 feet below the surface. The water there was in such abundance that Dr Mulik remarked, 'We can supply water to half of Mahabaleshwar!' Later a guest house was built there.

⚬⚭⚬

Parkhi Guruji, wearing a loincloth and an upper garment, approached me one day with a request. A gentleman called

Dalvi had donated him a piece of land in Nanded on Sinhgad Road in Poona. I dug a borewell for him there. He started the well-known Ved Pathshala (School for Vedic Studies) on the plot. He recalled a tale about Bhimanna.

'She' had once taken Bhimanna to Parkhi Guruji who was staying at Kasba Peth. 'She' was very interested in astrology. The guru possessed a *nadi-granth*, which contained the horoscopes of thousands of men and women detailed with forecasts. The relevant horoscope was located, it was read out, and Bhimanna paid the fees. The guru said, 'Anna, we will be grateful if you could sing a bhajan for us'. 'All right,' said Bhimanna and sonorous notes were struck, drawing in scores of neighbours. Bhimanna sang two more bhajans at their request.

The guru's son told me later what the horoscope had predicted. 'Guruji told me about the past of the maestro as follows: "Bhimsen was a fallen angel on Mount Kailash. Such people are not attracted to worldly life. They come to make people happy with their talent and then they return to Mount Kailash."'

I had no hesitation in believing this. I felt satisfied that I had been instrumental in bringing water to Parkhi Guruji's Ved Pathshala and Vedacharya Ghaisas Guruji's Ved Bhavan in Poona. I felt as if I had served my own grandfather, the Vedic scholar Guracharya.

In due course I learnt to drive the truck in the driver's absence. This acquainted me with the 'truck lingo' spoken by the drivers. Whenever the battery became weak I had to push-start the truck. Once I had to drive to a spot. After the work was over my workers tried to push-start the vehicle, but it would not budge. Finally when it did start to move it began to slide down the sloping road and the air brakes would not respond. I could not start the engine by shifting gears. Unless enough air pressure is built up by the engine the air brakes do not work. I was sweating profusely at the thought of what might happen if the vehicle were to crush someone. But after shifting the gear the engine started and the brakes also worked! I managed to divert the truck to a farm to avoid an accident. It was quite a traumatic experience for me.

I came home, slumped in a chair, drank a whole jug full of water, and signalled to my wife not to ask me any questions for a while. After some time, after calming down, I related the incident to her. If the truck had crushed someone or had turned turtle what would have been our fate, I thought to myself. The thought continued to perturb me for many days to come.

I had gone to Alibaug for drilling. On my way back I halted at my sister Sumangala's house at Jambhulpada where she was performing the housewarming ritual. After the ceremony I was driving back to Poona and many of my relatives, including members of my own family, were with me. When we reached Khandala ghat, the driver of the truck ahead of me suddenly braked. As a result I, too, had to stop. Being on a slope, I immediately asked my people to put stoppers at the rear wheels of the truck. Later when I tried to drive on, the truck could not negotiate the slope and it suddenly started sliding backwards, even jumping over the stoppers. My helpers carefully put stoppers again and the truck stopped sliding. I put the engine into the first gear and pressed the accelerator. The vehicle picked up speed and moved on! When we halted at Lonavala for a cup of tea, I was soaked in sweat. The others were not aware of what had happened. The truck could have easily landed into the valley just behind us!

The next ten years kept me busy neck-deep in my business and travelling. I could hardly keep track of Bhimanna's tours and concerts. We would meet sporadically and he would casually inquire about my progress. If I did not meet him for a long time, he would ring up in the early morning and say in his baritone, 'Is that Raghu? You haven't called for some time.' I would then make it a point to see him that very day, and it would be a memorable day for me. Once he asked me what gift he should bring for me and I asked for a wristwatch. He brought one for me from a foreign visit. While he was handing it over to me 'she' saw it. So I asked him if I was to pay for it. He shook his head implying 'no'. Once he brought me a good camera and I gave him the money in 'her' presence. He accepted it. I could easily read his mind and know his grief. It was painful for him; he was earning in lakhs and 'she' was squandering the wealth on her children leaving him without a right over his own earnings. I left his house teary-eyed; Mother lived with tears all her life. Our two homes were like two trains running parallel to one another: his, a Palace-on-Wheels, and ours, a passenger train!

Nine

I STOPPED GOING TO BHIMANNA for money on a monthly basis after I got a regular job. My younger brother Anand, who was slightly older than 'her' younger son, had to go to him for money needed for Mother's expenses. He had to suffer endless humiliations and angry outbursts. He could never get over the hurt and bitterness that Bhimanna's words caused in the presence of the 'other' family. Once he wanted to join a college trekking expedition and needed trekking shoes. When he went to ask for money he was humiliated in such rude language by Bhimanna that even his friend Dixit, who was present there and had told me the entire story, could not stomach it. 'Anna should not have done it,' he told me.

Bhimanna's 'other' family was squandering his money, including spending on their foreign visits. I could never understand how such a fine person could ever be so partial. When I was with him I crooned his favourite bhajan that went like 'Have compassion for your servants as much as for your sons',[1] but he got irritated and shouted, 'I've done everything for everyone'. The truth was that what he did for his servants he did not do for us—his own children. He even got a house for his servant using government quota. He was angry because he thought that I was hinting at such help for us too.

I had made it a practice to go to him and touch his feet before all important rituals and events. Once I went to see him on the auspicious day of Padva. My stepsister refused me entry into the house saying, 'He is busy giving tuitions'. I pushed my way past her and entered the room where he was teaching a couple of students—Kumar Gandharva's son being one of them—raga Abhogi. He was producing a difficult taan pattern which was a little beyond the learners' ability, but which I was confident of repeating. I had listened to his Abhogi several times earlier and knew the details by heart. Presently he came out of his trance and looked at me with a warm smile. I touched his feet and put a large *ramphal* (a variety of custard apple) from my garden at his feet. 'What fruit is this?' he asked. He said he had never eaten it before. I told him to let it ripen for a couple of days before eating it, and left. My stepsister had by then disappeared.

I went to him after a couple of days and casually asked if he had liked the ramphal. 'They kept it in a box and it rotted there,' he said. I was deeply hurt. This was possibly part of the plan to prevent him from feeling any love for us, I thought. 'All right,' he said, sadly. I shuddered to think how those evil people must have tortured Mother with similar wiles and guile.

∞‿∞

Grandfather Guracharya died in Gadag in 1982. Bhimanna was touring the USA then. His brothers performed the last rites. Though we could not make it to the funeral, Mother and I went to Gadag to offer condolences. Madhav Gudi told me that after Bhimanna's concert was over he asked him to send away all the others and stay alone with him. Then he broke down into profuse sobbing and recalled several of his incidents with his father. It is only natural for emotional lava to gush out on the passing away of such a near and dear relation. (In his book *Bhimsen*, Vasant Potdar has alleged that on that tour Bhimanna remained indifferent to his father's demise.)

I had heard a lot of stories about my grandfather's scholarship and love for discipline. He received his higher education (MA, BT-English) from Poona. Wrangler Paranjpe helped him during this time. He studied Sanskrit in Pandharpur and Gaya. He was the headmaster of a local school in Gadag and kept a strict watch on cheating in examinations. He would pretend to read a newspaper in which there was a hole through which he could keep an eye on the students.

He had a good command over English and Sanskrit, and conversed in Sanskrit with visiting scholars. He wrote several books in these two languages as well as in Kannada. In English he wrote Raghavendra Swami's biography along with study aids. In Kannada he wrote a book of fiction—an adventure story—and Bhimanna's biography, in which there was not a single reference to Bhimanna's second marriage. (Vasant Potdar has written that 'she' claimed that Guracharya had always showered blessings on 'her'.) He ran the Sanskrit Sadachar Pathshala (Sanskrit Good Behaviour School) for poor children and gave discourses on religious topics.

He did not visit Poona frequently, but when he did he made it a point to visit Mother and us. He was very pleased to see my own house at Dhayari. He would invariably reply to my letters.

Destiny has a role for everyone. It was Guracharya's destiny to father a gem like Bharat Ratna Bhimsen Joshi. In addition he also gave Bhimanna good health, genetically, a love of learning, a sharp intelligence, and a mind with great determination. This was by no means a small contribution and history cannot forget it, nor did Bhimanna himself forget it. The moment the word 'Appa' was mentioned, Bhimanna would pause for a while, feel moved, and recall an event or two about his father. It was these strong genes that had built Bhimanna, the doyen of Hindustani classical music.

In 1978 Mother was declared diabetic and suffering from hypertension. She responded well to treatment for some years, but developed cirrhosis of the liver. She began to spit blood and had to be admitted to hospital from time to time. Dr Ghaisas was always helpful. She would need blood and we had to run to the blood bank for it. My brother, children, and neighbours were always ready to help. Although Dr Ghaisas would diagnose her condition as 'critical' she would always return home cured. These visits were repeated at least twenty times until 1992.

Whenever she was admitted to the hospital I would inform Bhimanna. He always came to meet her and paid for the medical expenses. 'I see one advantage in this sickness,' Mother would joke. 'At least he comes to see me regularly!' She was a cheerful woman after all.

Once when Bhimanna came to meet her there was suddenly a commotion outside the hospital. Some children had gathered to see him. They wanted his autograph. He had become extremely popular after the release of the video in which he sang '*Mile sur mera tumhara, to sur bane hamara*' (When our notes are in harmony the whole world will be tuneful). Bhimanna signed willingly.

Mother passed away at the age of sixty-four on 14 April 1992. Many people came from Dhayari for the funeral. One of them, Ratnakar Kondhalkar, remarked fondly, 'How humane she was!'

Mother used to open her heart to my wife about her past and her sufferings. Despite the misfortunes she was forced to face, she had a sense of contentment. She had told my wife, 'Nothing much remains to wish for in my life now. I have children and grandchildren. I have eaten prasad from a banana leaf. I am his solemnly married wife. I am least bothered if dogs and wolves licked the leaf afterwards.' Bhimanna used to sing a bhajan *'Suno Lachhman pyare bhai'* (Listen, dear brother Lachhman) in which Rama tells his brother Lakshman that both happiness and sorrow are controlled by destiny.

Mother lived long enough to see my brother Anand's daughter Swarda, who was everybody's pet, daughters being dearly loved in the Joshi family. Anand's second child, a son, Tejas, was born later.

∞⧢∞

Bhimanna enjoyed good health even in his sixties. On a winter evening when his friend Dixit came to see him, Bhimanna came out of his room sweating. 'What's the matter?' he asked. 'Just did a couple of hundred push-ups. The body had stiffened. I feel great now,' said Bhimanna. Dixit was stunned. In his seventies, once while passing through Katraj ghat, his car got stuck in an open gutter. The driver needed a crane. But Bhimanna said, 'Hold the steering wheel, release the clutch, and kick the accelerator when I tell you.' Then he lifted the car from the rear and shouted, 'Kick!' And the car climbed out! Bhimanna was known for such feats since his childhood.

∞⧢∞

In 1982 Bhimanna stayed with Padmakar Khare in Dubai where he was working as a general manager. When I met Khare he told me in his wife's presence that she was his first love and Bhimanna's music, his second. But as soon as she went out of the room he said, 'In fact, it's the other way round!'

Khare was in a reminiscent mood. He recalled, 'Once Anna, a few of my friends, and I went to the gold market late at night. Such a group stroll was frowned upon by the local authorities, but we had some local magnates with us and hence we were safe. Within a few minutes, a crowd of some fifteen people started following us. Bhimanna turned around and asked them what the matter was. One of them said deferentially, 'We want nothing. Only, please visit our shops, we will feel blessed.'

Whichever shop Bhimanna stepped into, the shop owner presented him with a gold ring, or a medallion, or a necklace. Someone handed Khare a silver bowl to collect all the gifts; soon it was full to the brim. Bhimanna joked, 'The next time I will not come for a performance. I will come for a stroll only.' Everybody thoroughly enjoyed the joke.

When we were young, Bhimanna used to arrange for a taxi to bring us to the venue of the Sawai Gandharva Sangeet Mahotsav. Slowly this practice ceased. The organizers began to recognize me only after my business started to flourish. Earlier whenever we went there, Dr Nanasaheb Deshpande would rush forward to meet us and pat us. Even so, an officious man in charge of the seating arrangements always looked down on me, although Bhimanna had got a job for his 'mediocre son'.

Once we attended the festival along with the members of my family and my brothers-in-law as Bhimanna's special guests. This officious man came to me and said, 'You have to move to that place'. There were no chairs where he pointed. I was at the end of my patience and said a little loudly, 'We won't shift. Tell Anna.' Dr Gokhale, one of the organizers, rushed to me and asked, 'What's the trouble, Raghu?' It was, after all, the voice of Bhimanna's son, loud and bold! At this moment Bhimanna himself came to us and spoke in Kannada. He took away our passes and placed tickets for special seats in our hands. The officious man was crestfallen.

All through our childhood we had been subjected to humiliation and deprivation. There is a limit to everything. Parasites have no self-respect. Although Bhimanna sent us tickets the 'others' saw to it that we were allotted seats at the back of the theatre. I had to tell one of the hangers-on to behave and learn to respect others. 'We are the real progeny of Bhimanna's happy moments!' The hanger-on was greatly put off at hearing my words.

∞∞∞

I expanded my house in Dhayari as my children were grown-up and were now attending college. An extra bedroom was added with a staircase leading to the terrace. During this time the residents of Dhayari organized a Dnyaneshwari Reading Week, to which a celebrated speaker was invited to give a religious discourse every day. A group bhajan was also organized. The organizers went to Bhimanna for a bhajan performance, but he declined as he had other engagements. They then came to me asking me to persuade him. I requested Bhimanna and also told him that the people of Dhayari had helped me rise in life. My borewell work had started from this place itself. Bhimanna readily agreed and asked for no honorarium. I told the organizers to treat him with the dignity he deserved. I hosted a dinner at my place after the bhajan.

Bhimanna came with his full retinue—'she', her daughter, daughter-in-law, and others. It was part of their strategy not to let Bhimanna be alone with us. He prayed to Lord Shiva in the temple and stepped onto the stage. It was a pleasant

141

evening with a cool breeze blowing and the place was packed with audience. It was a grand performance thoroughly enjoyed by everyone. After the concert was over I asked him and his guests to join us for dinner. He took me aside and said, 'I have got many people with me. I hope you can manage.' 'Yes, there will be no problem even if ten more were to join us,' I replied. He felt a little uncomfortable because he had not informed us in advance about the large number of people coming with him.

As we were proceeding to the terrace where the dinner was arranged, 'she' stopped in front of Mother's portrait and said, 'Instead of this photograph you should put up one of her in her young days'. We were stunned. This woman had destroyed Mother's youth and was now adding insult to injury. Bhimanna rested in the bedroom for a while. The whole house was fragrant with the sweet smell of *jui* flowers in the garden. He said, 'What a lovely sensation!' I was beside myself with joy to see him so happy in my house.

I had arranged a menu with ten of his favourite dishes. We were pleased as everyone greatly enjoyed the food. Even after years Tulshidas Borkar remembered how tasty the curd-rice was! It could not but be so as it was lavishly laced with cream. My children Rahul and Atul, and my nephew Girish, served the guests with great enthusiasm. We had never been invited to Bhimanna's place for any function. 'She' had intentionally avoided bringing her sons to the treat. It was likely that the elder one was 'flying' (to use Bhimanna's favourite term for being under the influence of stimulating liquid) and the younger one was studiously kept away from us. No compromise on apishness!

Even after I had built my own house and renovated it once nobody from their side visited us except Bhimanna. And he was very happy. For a long while he enjoyed sitting on the cane swing in the sit-out on the first floor. He used to croon looking at the newly sprouting trees in the yard. By nature he was a man of few words.

∞∞∞

Ramakantkaka suggested that I should perform a puja of the family deity, Lord Narasimha. Accordingly the arrangements began. I requested Bhimanna to spare the day for us. We invited his brothers Narayankaka and Vyankanna as well. Ramakantkaka brought from Dharwad the images of Dhwadd Devaru, the Great God. Guru Kittur Achar and his daughter Gayatri—my aunt—also came specially to supervise everything. The celebration was to be a grand event.

Image after image was taken out of the case made of deer hide. They were given the sacred ablution, and the mantras were sung sonorously. We sat on one side watching the whole ritual. Bhimanna sat on a swing, deep in reflection. It was fifty-four years after his marriage with my mother that he was meeting the family deities.

They were beautiful images cast in a five-metal mould, and had been worshipped in the Joshi family for the last 250 years. They included Lakshmi, Narasimha, and Prandev (Maruti), among others. I offered a small *mukut* (tiara) to Lord Narasimha. Damodarkaka's son Vasudev also came for the puja. Narayankaka's son Sanjay came all the way from the USA. The puja continued for two hours. At the end the rice offering was performed. Narayankaka signalled to me to ask Bhimanna to sing a prayer. Bhimanna intercepted the look and declared that he would not sing. Then, within a moment, he started reciting mantras in pure Sanskrit and continued for almost twenty minutes. This done, Narayankaka and Vyankanna also recited mantras and offered flowers to the gods.

143

I remember the scene in great detail even today and my hair stands on end. I regretted not having a tape recorder. A great chance to record mantras chanted sonorously by the children of the Vedic scholar Guracharya was lost. Bhimanna and Narayankaka sat on a couch and Vyankanna sat at their feet. Narayankaka asked him why he was sitting on the floor. Pat came the answer, 'That is where Hanuman always sits!' That was his Rama worship! He dearly loved Bhimanna.

After the puja was over Bhimanna asked me, 'Do you need me to help you with some money?' I said, 'By your grace and the grace of God, I have enough to fend for myself.' While he was reclining on the swing, my friend Jayant Badve asked him about my singing. Bhimanna exclaimed, 'Raghu? He will continue after me!' I was stunned and failed to see what he meant.

Bhimanna's cousin (Bandekaka's son) Sunil Joshi, the test cricketer, came for prasad in the evening. He was following a strict diet, but he could not resist the temptation of Alphonso mangoes. 'Her' children did not turn up. This was a rare opportunity to see the family deities, but perhaps they thought of it as mere ritualism and saw no gold in it!

I often think that Bhimanna played multiple roles in a single birth. While in the math of Raghavendra Swami, he would be in a trance. The way he bowed before the swami's *vrindavan*, he seemed the very image of devoutness. Raghavendra Swami worshipped Lord Rama; Bhimanna worshipped the Rama in his musical notes! He would always begin a concert by sitting still in meditation for a minute and then commence.

When his own bungalow was constructed, and the house-warming was to take place, his father asked him if the family gods were to be brought to the new house. Bhimanna declined. He was aware of 'her' view of the Joshi family deities. Besides, he did not want the family gods to be neglected by anyone in his own house. Mother and we were not invited for the ceremony.

Several new housing societies were coming up in Poona in those days and Bhimanna, on the strength of his standing in society, could have easily arranged for a small residential flat for us. He did not do it. 'She' had made it clear to him that she would not allow any pampering of our family.

After the housewarming puja was over and Guracharya was to leave for Gadag, Bhimanna asked Dixit to buy a good shawl for him. When 'she' was listening to his words 'she' immediately told Dixit, 'Don't get an expensive one'. When recounting the story to me, Dixit said that as they were leaving, Bhimanna gestured to him to buy a really expensive one!

∽∾

My brother Anand and I planted several fruit trees on our plot at Dhayari, and watered the plot using with water from a handpump. Even now we enjoy all the delicious fruits from these trees. The grafted-mango tree gives ample juicy fruits, tiring us all out as we pick them during the season. The first coconut plucked from high up the tree was like finding the exact high note of a raga! Bhimanna was greatly pleased with my Alphonso mangos, chikus, and bananas. I used to offer the season's first fruits to him with the same sense of reverence as I did to our gods. He would always signal 'Excellent!' It was an incomparable joy for me. But, of course, this response is natural only to the legitimately born children. Parasites are not capable of cherishing such small joys.

I also bought a cow, but it gave milk only during a couple of months in a year. I used to tie it up within my compound.

Once when I was trying to secure it, it managed to escape and I had to keep chasing it. It entered an adjoining farm and ate to its heart's fill. The neighbour was a thorough gentleman and did not mind the damage to his crop. The very next day I gifted the cow to our milkman. I cannot forget the taste of the sweets Mother had made from that cow's milk.

The entire area is now crowded with tall residential buildings, but it has not lost its former peace and calm. I enjoy watering my plants hours on end. When the *akashmogra* bursts into blossom, the air fills with the scented of its fragrance, and then I remember how, once upon a time, the whole stretch was a piece of barren land. In a short article published in a local paper, I had said that pure music can emanate from a mind that has fed on pure nature. I now experience the same feeling when I stand near my trees. All the tensions and trials vanish when I lean against the trunk of this great friend of mine, the akashmogra tree.

~

1. *Je ka ranjale ganjale, tyasi mhane jo apule*
    To chi sadhu olakhawa
    Dev tethechi janawa.
    Daya karane je putrasi
    Techi dasa ani dasi
    Tuka mhane sangu kiti
    Techi Bhagwantachi murti.

(One who owns and accepts those who are downtrodden and suffering, is the real sadhu in whom God is to be seen. The same compassion which the father has for his son, should be extended to the servants as well. Tuka says that he need not explain that such a person is the very image of God.)

Ten

WHEN BHIMANNA ABANDONED US and went to Nagpur from Badami, he had written a letter to Mother in Kannada. It was replete with a deep sense of regret. He had written, *I have wronged you deeply. I am caught in a vicious net. But I promise that I will never disown you and the children. Please forgive me.* Long after my sisters, Sumangala and Usha, and I had got married, Mother showed the letter to my wife Maya and said, 'Now that the children are married, why should I keep this letter?' And she tore it into pieces. My wife, too, was not mature enough to understand the importance of preserving such documents.

The restrictions on Bhimanna's liberty got progressively stricter, so much so that he would refuse to recognize us at concerts if 'she' was around. He was forced to prevent all information about his first marriage and children from appearing in any public medium. We realized how slavish he had become when he suppressed all reference to his first marriage in a documentary made on him by the eminent cine-writer Gulzar. My two children—Bhimanna's grandsons—were college-going young lads then. How humiliated they must have felt to be left unacknowledged like this!

Once Bhimanna was to meet a friend of mine from England. He asked me to see him at his relative's place at Deccan Gymkhana in Poona. When I reached there, my friend was not at home. The host introduced me as Bhimanna's son to the people in the house, but the mistress of the house blared, 'Maybe, but I know everyone and everything at Bhimanna's place from "her".' I was stunned more by the indecent curiosity about 'everything' in other people's houses than by the refusal to accept me for who I was. I left without reacting and waited downstairs at the door. Whenever I come across such a lack of sensitivity, I remember Bhimanna's favourite bhajan by Sant Kabir '*Sab paise ke bhai*' (Everybody claims relationship with the moneyed).

Bhimanna was once suffering from common cold and took a strong course of antibiotics to get rid of it before a performance, but it made him weak. His voice sounded like coming from the depth of a well. He held my hand for a while. As the 'others' were around, he spoke to me only through this touch. 'Get well,' I said, pressing his hand, and left.

He was getting old and caution demanded that the number of performances he gave be limited. In 1996, he fell from the staircase and hurt his spine. For over a month he was bedridden. Again in 1998 he had a fall and broke both his knees. Added to the problem was the high dosage of antibiotics which confined him, alone and sad, to his bed upstairs. I met him frequently.

One evening when I was with him, the attendant left us. All around lay mounds of litter and junk, making the room look like an attic. Next to his pillow stood a framed photograph of Bhimanna's father and that of God Maruti of Yalgur near Bijapur. I had crossed fifty, and we were with each other, all by ourselves, after years. So I boldly asked him a question that had rankled me all these years.

I asked for permission and said, 'Bhimanna, when you sing Abhogi or Jogiya or Bhairavi, you make the audiences weep. How, then, can you be so hard-hearted with me and with all of us?' Tears began to trickle from his eyes as he tightened his grip on my hand and whispered, 'If you allow someone else to pull your strings, then life is only a cacophony!' He had understood perfectly the question to which I sought an answer. He was trying to tell me that the greatest loss in such a situation was the loss of one's freedom. I was surprised that such a strong person should sound so depressed. My own grief came from the fact that while he gave everything to everyone so generously, he withheld his music from me. His answer was contained in a short sentence, but there was no end to our suffering.

As I left to go down the servant came and said to Bhimanna, 'Ask your students to come here and sing. It will be a good recreation for you.' I stopped, turned around, and asked Bhimanna, 'Shall I sing a bhajan for you?' 'Go ahead.' As I shut the door he asked, 'Why shut it?' 'If I am out of tune, let it not trouble others,' I answered. Then I sang 'Teerth Vitthal, kshetra Vitthal'. After many years I had got the opportunity to sing in his presence. When I finished the song, he held my hand and pressed it gently as tears flowed down his cheeks. I had poured my heart and soul into the singing as he used to. He was touched.

My elder son Rahul got married in March 1998. As Bhimanna was bedridden, he could not attend the wedding. The veteran vocalist Gangubai Hangal and her daughter Krishna had gone to see him. Since the nurse was sponging him we waited in the living room. The place was a model of mismanagement with sundry things lying higgledy-piggledy. 'How many rooms are there at the top?' asked Krishna. 'I know only the sanctum sanctorum, that is, Bhimanna's room. I haven't seen the whole of his—my father's—bungalow,' I said.

Selecting a birthday gift for Bhimanna was always a challenge for me. Usually I gave him Nehru silk shirts that snuggled close to his body. He would point to it before starting his performance. Often it used to be a heart-to-heart communication without the interference of words.

The engagement ceremony of my younger son Atul, with Leena whom he was in love with, was arranged in Hotel Shreyas in Poona in October 1998. Bhimanna was present right through though his face showed clear signs of exhaustion. A few days later I got a call from a servant in Bhimanna's house telling me that he was unwell and was being shifted to the King Edward Memorial Hospital. He had specifically asked the servant to inform me. Hence the call. I rushed to the hospital. Half a dozen doctors attended to him in the ICU. An abdominal ulcer had burst and he was in shock. He returned to normalcy after a couple of hours' struggle, and was moved to the operation room. As he was being shifted he said to me in Kannada, 'I am going now'. Again I was traumatized. After a couple of hours, however, Dr Subhash Patki sent out word that the surgery had been successful and Bhimanna was out of danger.

I visited him the next day when he was moved to a private room. 'Her' younger son guarded the door. 'Is the doctor in?' I asked. 'Hmm ...' was the reply. After waiting for about fifteen minutes I entered the room. There lay Bhimanna, fully awake and alert. 'How are you now?' I asked him. 'Excellent,' he answered with a smile. Just then a nurse entered and shouted at me, 'Please get out!' I kept quiet for a minute and answered with equal force, 'Do you have any idea who I am? I am his eldest son.' She kept quiet and I left instantly. I knew who had instigated her; even so I restrained myself and continued to visit him in the hospital. A couple of days later the same nurse said, 'Sir, please visit him every day. I have noted that he speaks only with you. Not a word with the others.' When the physiotherapist wanted Bhimanna to get up and try to walk a little, he showed no response. Then I said to him in Kannada, 'Why are you so stubborn? Come on, I'll take you.' Instantly he got up, had a stroll around the ward, and came back all fresh. The doctor said, 'You'd better come every day.' I agreed and did visit him every day.

Bhimanna disliked the Kannada–Marathi controversy. He never thought of them as two separate languages. He would not allow a Kannadiga to speak ill of Marathi; in the company of Marathi speakers he would declare that though he was a Marathi, it was not necessary to add that he was not a Kannadiga! It was all transparent and clean to him. 'My notes are neither Kannada nor Marathi. I see to it that they touch the inner chords of my audience. That's what matters.' That is why when the Karnataka Ratna award was being conferred on him in 2005, Bhimanna got annoyed when some reporters asked the minister to speak in Marathi. He said, 'Damn it! These Kannada–Marathi fellows are here too!' However, he was not allowed to speak much as he was suffering from a new tumour that was developing in his brain. Meanwhile, the 'young prince' had grabbed the mike. I can only state that the eminent Kannada writer S.L. Bhyrappa is respected by Marathi-speaking people and that many Marathi plays have been a favourite with Kannada audiences. A language should communicate and connect.

When I next visited the hospital to see Bhimanna, my stepbrother, 'her' elder son, stood guarding the door. Bhimanna was to be discharged in the afternoon and my stepbrother requested me to help him take Bhimanna to his home in his car. As the car entered the gate of his house, his retinue gathered around. While Bhimanna was getting out of the car he lost control of his bowels and his clothes got soiled. No one came forward to help. I asked for some toilet paper, cleaned Bhimanna's feet and slippers, took him to the washroom, cleaned him completely, and took him to his bed. All this while my stepsister was shouting at the nurse for not cleaning him. The nurse simply answered that she could not do it. My stepsister's anger clearly stemmed out of a desire to prevent any love blooming for me in Bhimanna's mind! That was how 'she' had groomed the children. However, I was deeply grateful that I had been of some help to my revered father in his moment of need. (Potdar's book *Bhimsen* describes this incident, but without referring to me!)

Bhimanna was losing control of his bodily functions due to the growing left frontal meningioma, a tumour of the brain. This ailment once led him into a fit of forgetfulness when he was performing at the Pune Ganesh Festival. However, the audience accepted him as he was.

After he recovered from the surgery for the removal of tumor in 1998, he gave his first performance at the University of Pune on 2 February 2002. Gangubai Hangal was among the audience. Sitar maestro Bhaskar Chandavarkar spoke extremely well about Bhimanna's music. He observed, 'Today, when there is a surfeit of cultural aggression in art, Bhimsen Joshi's bastion of classical singing stands undisturbed, undented, unaffected.' Bhimanna too spoke pithily, 'A singer has to develop his own vision'. Vocalist Shaila Datar, standing by my side, was visibly moved listening to him.

He had to relieve himself before starting his performance. As he made a move towards the washroom, I came forward to help him. He stopped me and remarked. 'Several others are following to support me'. This was a reference to the home retinue. I withdrew. I could guess that he was reluctant because he must have been given a severe telling-off after I had washed him on the previous occasion. He had been strictly warned not to acknowledge our presence in public. Else why would he be so curt with me? How would one feel if one's beloved refused to take cognizance of one? On such occasions I would invariably remember Bhimanna's favourite Bhairavi: *'Boli na bol humse piya sang ... hum sang laagi preet, un sang karao sukh chain man rang nit, naam machao rumjhum ...'* (O my love, you don't speak with me ... you love me but you enjoy 'her' company, turbulent emotions perturb my mind).

When my younger son Atul was to get married, I telephoned Bhimanna that I wished to see him. 'Come late tomorrow morning,' he said. I went to his place at one in the afternoon when he, too, was just entering the house. 'How can they refuse when I put in a word?' he asked as he took off his jacket. When he saw the puzzled look on my face he said, 'The younger one bought a pistol from Calcutta, but the police refused to issue a licence. I had to see the officer. The documents came through. But, then, what is the use of a pistol if fifty men attack you?' Yes I, too, fail to understand the use of a weapon in art. Is it for those who refuse to listen to you?

Atul and Leena got married in March 1999. Bhimanna was present throughout. All our near and distant relations had gathered, among whom there were Godu Aji, Narayankaka, and Vyankanna. It was an affectionate family gathering and my son's in-laws, Bankubhai Gujjar and his wife Meenatai, looked after everybody's comforts willingly and affectionately.

Atul and Leena had a son Pranav on 2 March 2002, making me a grandfather and Bhimanna a great-grandfather. I wanted to have the customary ceremony of showering gold flowers with Pranav sitting in his great-grandfather Bhimanna's lap.

Bhimanna agreed readily. Atul and Leena washed Bhimanna's feet and put Pranav on his lap. Flowers of pure gold were showered on their heads. Bhimanna was silent all this while. When my wife requested Bhimanna to have his meal he said, 'Raghu, too, wants me to eat. Let's all eat together. I have all the time for you today.' I was content when I fed Bhimanna with my hands. I could sense in his voice his deep desire to be among his own family. Blood had become thicker than water at least for some hours.

When Bhimanna was operated upon for the brain tumour, only one person was allowed to visit him at a time. When I went to see him at the hospital 'her' sister's husband was sitting with him and showed no signs of moving out. Finally I went in and asked him to leave as I wanted to say something personal to Bhimanna, who cheered up, and became chatty when he saw me. He went into a reminiscent mood and recounted the fun times of the old days with his maternal uncle at Badami. He soon returned home, but it took a long time for him to recover his normal health. The scar on his forehead showed clearly. When I met him he remarked, 'All is frigid everywhere. I have to resume.' He was hinting at his empty coffers. I replied coolly, 'There is plenty of fuel. No need to keep adding to it in your present condition.' He gave me a sad smile.

Bhimanna's friend Ram Pujari came around with two members of his trust. He said, 'Don't exhaust yourself. Don't give many performances now.' Pointing at the Dobermann chained close by Bhimanna retorted, 'If I don't earn, they will tie me along with him.' Everybody was shocked and fell silent, as the trustees told me later.

The fact was that Bhimanna was quite wealthy. He had been granted a spacious flat by the government in the posh Lokhandwala complex in Bombay, and he owned a flat in

Bangalore as well. A lot of money had come in from their sale. Even so he was hammered continuously with only one tune, 'We are broke. How can we live if you don't perform?' No one else in the house ever thought of earning for a living.

When the *shehnai* maestro Bismillah Khan was in financial straits the government had come forward to look after him. Bhimanna's comment was, 'There are fifty parasites in his family. An artist must provide for his own future.' It was ironic that what he expected others to do for themselves, he easily neglected in his own case. The fact is that he was not aware of how well he was earning.

In private conversations Bhimanna would often complain, 'These people have turned me into a circus bear. I have to ride the bike when they order and start making the rounds (sing)!' It was a kind of bonded labour. He was thoroughly exploited, financially and emotionally. But a different, made-up facade was presented to the world. It was like controlling a huge elephant with a small goad. Although he was completely exhausted, he was made to perform even twice a day. Sometimes he had to be taken lying down in the car, wailing and moaning all the way. His accompanists were witness to his suffering. He was invited by Sharad Pawar to perform at Baramati. The family doctor was worried whether Bhimanna could sit for a long time, and shared the concern with his family. The rueful answer was, 'How can we give up two lakh rupees?'

When Bhimanna was admitted into Sahyadri Hospital for spine surgery, I noticed that one of his toes had become rigid. When I pointed it out to the nurse who had looked after him for years, she said that the toe had been like that for the past thirty years. It had become bent by stepping on the car clutch. I was not convinced, so I bought a corn cap and asked her to fit it over the toe. Within a week the toe became normal.

I was happy to look after his physical well-being. When he was shifted to his room I went to see him with prasad from Raghavendra Swami's math. He was seated on his bed and looked fresh. 'How are you?' he asked me. 'I am well. Shall I sing a bhajan for you?' I asked. 'Certainly!' he exclaimed. I sang *'Yeh tanu mundna be mundna, aakhir mitti mein mil jana'* (Adorn your body, for it will finally merge into the soil one day). He was happy and conveyed it to the nurse standing just behind me. It was certainly a difficult composition in raga Bhairavi. That day I returned home with a matchless sense of fulfilment to see him pleased with my performance.

Bhimanna's fans loved and thoroughly enjoyed his performances. But how many of them knew what agonies Bhimanna suffered in the last ten years of his life? After all the body has its own limits and a decline is inevitable. His friend Dixit once paid him a visit during his illness. He asked, 'Any pain in the body?' Bhimanna asked him to come closer and whispered in his ear, 'How can I show you where it hurts? It hurts all over!' The smile that followed was clearly touched with sorrow. When Dixit recounted the story to me, I could not help visualizing him as a stick of sugar cane from which the last drop of juice was being extracted. But, then, I was helpless as he was practically under house arrest during his last years. Even the celebrities who wished to meet him had the same impression.

When Bhimanna came home from Sahyadri Hospital he had to use a wheelchair, and needed a support under his arms and for his neck. When I visited him he was sitting in it, almost in a stupor. The 'young prince' sat in front of him, asking him to teach him a particular raga. The prince sang in snatches. How ecstatic Bhimanna must have felt at the 'divine' performance!

During another visit I saw him sitting in his wheelchair, but the supports were missing. He would cry loudly if he did not have them, so I adjusted the pillows, cleaned his face, and touched his feet. He was praying to Lord Rama. The TV was blaring loudly in front of him, spouting some news about a bar dancer found with a lot of cash in her possession. No conversation was possible amid such a din. Bhimanna asked 'her' to lower the volume, but his request fell on deaf ears. He smiled piteously. This was how he was treated in his own home. Here was a man whom the whole world respected, but was condemned to total negligence at home. But that's how the weak are made to pay!

Bhimanna's room beats all description! The paint on the walls was peeling off. A thick mattress lay on the floor without being dusted for years. In fact it reeked as if food droppings had seeped into it. The stench got stronger on rainy days. Spools of music recorded by young vocalists aspiring to perform at the Sawai Gandharva Sangeet Mahotsav had piled up over time. There were countless holes in his shawl. Ash from incense sticks accumulated over weeks lay heaped in a pot. Old papers were piled in a corner. When Bhimanna was well he used to see to it that the room was kept clean, neat, and tidy. He would destroy old papers. No one bothered about the upkeep now that Bhimanna had become an invalid. Eventually the dirty mattress was replaced with a mat at the suggestion of the doctor who had also advised adult diapers which, however, were not bought as they were costly. The nurse was asked to make do with the old, used ones.

Once 'she' discovered that a diamond-studded box was missing. The suspicion fell on a housemaid. However, despite Bhimanna's personal influence with the police, the box was never found. That is how, in trying to grab everything, one sometimes loses precious possessions.

Bhimanna was hospitalized when 'she' died. I was with him, but he was not in a state to bear the news. 'Don't allow anyone to see him,' I was told by the 'others'. A private nurse attended on him and used to bring home-cooked food for him. This time sweet porridge had been sent for him. When the nurse asked to be allowed to leave in order to pay her last respects to the deceased, I requested her to come back quickly as I too wished to attend the cremation. I had brought with me some food for him as I knew how thoughtful the 'other' people were in such matters! They did not know that eating sweets is a sacrilege during mourning, and unthinkable in the Joshi clan.

After the nurse returned I went to the crematorium to pay my respects. I had been groomed in a tradition which regards it as indecent not to respect the dead. Dixit was present there. As Bhimanna himself was absent the funeral was attended sparsely. His window in Sahyadri Hospital commanded a view of the crematorium, but he was not aware of 'her' demise. Inscrutable are the ways of destiny!

I was keenly reminded of Mother's funeral. She died on 14 April 1992. I had given Bhimanna some idea of her health, so he visited her in Gore Hospital before leaving for Bombay. He became serious when he saw how she was gasping for breath. I tried to draw her attention to him, but she looked at him vacantly. Maybe she saw nothing but her death. She died the same evening. I telephoned Bhimanna to inform him of her passing away. 'I can't come. Perform the last rites.' 'I knew that's what you would say ...' I broke down. Within ten minutes he called back to say, 'Hold the funeral, I am reaching tomorrow morning'.

158

The funeral procession left from my home in Dhayari; hundreds stood in silence and joined the procession. My sons made the pyre while Bhimanna looked on. He put a kumkum mark on her forehead as his farewell to her. As I stoked the dying flames, I remembered what Mother often used to say in her last days: 'I have a sense of fulfilment. My children and grandchildren are as good as gold. I will die as a legitimate wife with my husband's kumkum on my forehead.' For most of her life, she had never had the good fortune to be respected as Bhimanna's wife. But at least he was present when she left us forever. That was her final triumph, and no one could ever deprive her of it.

As I was washing my feet after the cremation a hand patted my back affectionately. It was Bhimanna's hand touching the very spot where I have a tuft of hair—a family feature coming down to me from Grandfather Guracharya! Not since my birth had he touched me with so much affection!

I performed all the death rites for Mother and Bhimanna attended throughout. He even gave a substantial donation in her name at the Raghavendra Swami math. On the thirteenth day of mourning he came to my house and sat silently with a vacant expression on his face. How I wished that he had given some time to Mother, for she did not expect much from him to be happy. I was told that Bhimanna wept profusely at the math. Those were tears of repentance from one who was so sensitive, so cultured but, at the same time, so helpless, caught up as he was in the coils of misfortune.

The following month he performed an elaborate puja at the math, rode in Lord Rama's holy chariot with me, and distributed fruits all around.

Eleven

BHIMANNA OFTEN USED TO MEET me and my wife at Raghavendra Swami's math. Once it happened that my wife's younger sister Akalpita also accompanied us. As per custom Bhimanna stood with the *arati* (a ritual of blessing or welcoming someone) in his hands and my wife and Akalpita stood behind him. The arati over, Bhimanna turned around, put the sacred coconut in my wife's hands, and blessed both as the two sisters touched his feet. He would be very informal and affectionate on such occasions and never flaunted his celebrity status. Later my wife asked her, 'Did you feel any vibes?' She said that she had sensed a kind of beautiful aura around her. Many a time even I have experienced his aura, which possibly emanated from the music he had in his soul.

Once when I was at the math he was also present, and after the arati he sat in a chair. Whenever he was in Poona he would visit the math on Thursdays, escorted by someone. He continued this practice till the end. I sat near him when he beckoned to me. As we were talking about each other's well-being, a middle-aged woman came, touched his feet, and started crying bitterly. The whole atmosphere became tense for a few minutes. Bhimanna asked her what was wrong. She said, 'My husband was in the merchant navy and I used to be with him on the ship for months together. Sometimes the loneliness haunted us, but Anna your singing was a great relief for us.

160

When I saw you here today I could not resist speaking to you. I am a lucky person today. Anna, please bless me.' Bhimanna smiled gently and said, 'Be happy. All will be well.'

I am not promoting idolatry, but I have known and seen people looking upon Bhimanna as a saintly figure. His music always drove away one's melancholy and pessimism. A young Bengali woman once recounted a similar experience to me when I was travelling to Udaipur. Her husband, too, was in the navy. It was Bhimanna's notes that had charmed James Beverage from across the waters.[1]

Later some biographers of Bhimanna's wrote that he was nothing without 'her'. It was as if the years he had spent with his parents, with Mother, and with us counted for nothing. Most of these biographies are full of cooked-up tales.

When Bhimanna's ulcer burst, his brother Vyankanna was in the same house. However, when he tried to see Bhimanna he was denied entry into the room and was, in fact, pushed aside with, 'You may be his brother or whatever....' He dashed against a chair and hurt his ear which was permanently damaged. His wife, Leelakaku, never allowed him to visit Bhimanna by himself thereafter.

What an uncultured way of behaving towards one's elders! If Bhimanna had been in his usual health he would surely have taught the miscreants a good lesson. When his own father died without assigning a single room in the house to his younger son Madhav, Bhimanna felt hurt. 'It was unjust on Father's part,' he said. I gave him a suggestive look meaning, 'What, then, should you have done for us?' He sensed the irony, dodged the issue, and said, 'But, of course, Father must have had his own reasons! Family customs demand that even the curses of elders are to be respected as blessings!' I was thoroughly nonplussed, but he only smiled.

In reality, he used to feel guilty and was perturbed that, in spite of his immense wealth, he was unable to help his own people and progeny. 'I am solely responsible for this state of affairs,' he would tell his student Madhav Gudi. Unlike Sinbad, who could eventually throw off the old man clinging to his back, Bhimanna, unfortunately, continued to carry 'her' around his neck till the very end. He was no longer healthy and was, in fact, an invalid towards the end. But 'she' and, after her, her progeny clung on.

During those painful days I met Bhimanna at his place. The driver told me that he had asked me to come to his room. He was bedridden. I bowed before him and handed over his favourite poha chivda and laddus to the driver. Bhimanna seemed in good spirits and said to me in Hindi, *'Kitna karte ho mere liye!'* (You do so much for me). I answered in Hindi, 'So what! Yayati's son gave up his youth for his father. I would have given up my life for the happiness of your fans.' 'Be happy,' he smiled. I knew that the writer V.S. Khandekar had given a complimentary copy of his novel *Yayati* to Bhimanna, and he had read it.

Once when I went to see Bhimanna the house was bolted from outside to prevent the 'flying' son from escaping. Ganesh, the servant, ushered me into the room. Bhimanna was sitting in a reverie in his chair in front of the TV. I touched his feet, sat close to him, and fed him prasad from the swami's math. After a while he looked at me and said, 'It's sad Saraswati Rane is no more'. She was a music maestro and his contemporary. I noticed that his hand was bandaged. It was a little blue in colour, and looked like a roasted brinjal. I asked him what the matter was. He kept quiet. The driver told me that the heater kept close to him had scorched his hand. How uncared for he was! I felt deeply upset.

The next time I went to see him the door was latched from both sides as usual. I was allowed in; Bhimanna was watching Animal Planet. The huge face of a lion with an abundant mane filled the whole screen. Bhimanna had once been like that lion, but now he was without teeth and claws. 'Which dish made by your mother was your favourite?' I asked him only to activate his recall power. '*Methkut*' (spiced gram powder), he replied quickly.

While in Sahyadri Hospital he asked his driver to get him onion bhaji. He always blessed everyone with a '*Khush raho!*' (Be happy), though he himself always tried to be happy.

The Joshi family has a long tradition of assembling at the Narasimha temple at M.K. Hubli near Belgaum every May to offer a puja to the family deities. Once a barren place, this spot has now become beautiful with proper upkeep. The legend goes that Sage Chyavana prayed here for years and is said to have researched on *amla* (gooseberries). While the traditional pilgrims go into the temple to pray, the young ones of the clan, clad in loincloths, even play cricket. At the end a mega puja is offered when everyone has to be present with flowers in hand.

I, too, bow my head where Bhimanna, his father, and his forefathers have also prayed. I do not like to challenge anyone's beliefs and I don't indulge in dry rationalism. All of us have our breakfast of laddus and poha and our family priest offers us prasad after he has performed the puja. Then we glut ourselves on the traditional feast of sweet milk porridge and *manda*s (paper-thin chapatti of fine wheat flour, sugar, and ghee) with a liberal dollop of ghee on them! At such times the whole family is closely knit with bonds of affection. Everyone draws upon memories of elders and the bygone good old days, and tears well up in their eyes.

After Bhimanna was honoured with the Bharat Ratna I was in M.K. Hubli at the puja offered to Dhwadd Devaru. The family priest held every divine image high up so that it could be seen by all and then wrapped them up in a silk cloth. A number of cameras clicked when he hoisted the image of Lord Narasimha. My eyes became moist as I saw Bhimanna himself in the Lord's image. Immediately I called Bhimanna who was in Poona and reported to him all the details of the puja. He said, 'The Lord has put me where I am today. Give my namaskar to the Lord.' Bhimanna himself has now become the Dhwadd Devaru for the entire Joshi clan!

Newspapers flashed the news that Dr A.P. J. Abdul Kalam, the then president of India, was scheduled to meet Bhimanna in Poona. My love for him and my pride in him knew no bounds.

The American presidents used to go to visit Carver, renowned agricultural scientist, at his house. My father was of the same stature as Carver, whose magic touch could turn the most barren plot into a lush green field full of flowers, fruits, and vegetables. Bhimanna could turn into gold whatever notes he picked up to perform. His voice had that alchemic touch.

Next day I went to see Bhimanna he was in session with his physiotherapist. He relaxed in a wheelchair after the regimen was over. It was an exhausting experience for him, but there was no other way out. After a few minutes he turned to me with a 'Hmm....' This was a cue for me to talk to him. I bent before him, caressed his feet, and said the prayer '*Shree Rama jai Rama jai jai Rama*' (Praise to Lord Rama), which he repeated. This was the usual understanding between us, but I derived immense joy and gained a rare sensation from it. Physically, Bhimanna was a completely broken man, but his inner, spiritual strength was sterling bright. A mere glance at him convinced me of it.

He moved his head gently to indicate 'How are you?' I went closer to him, cleaned medicine stains still visible on his face with a napkin, adjusted his urine bag, and stood close to him. I always cherished such moments of physical closeness with him. Then I caressed his hair and asked, 'How do you feel now?' Instead of the usual answer he said, *'Kuchh theek nahin hai'* (Nothing seems to be okay). Then he turned his gaze to the ceiling and said, 'I'm just waiting'. 'That's all right. I am told the president, Dr Kalam, is going to visit you soon,' I replied. 'Yes. He's an old friend of mine.' After a few other exchanges I asked, 'Can I be present on the occasion?' He was visibly nervous and said, 'No way. A list of names has been already sent to the authorities. They do not want a crowd.' I had touched a sore point. I met his gaze for a moment and he understood how I felt. Clearly he had been properly briefed in the matter. 'It's okay,' I said, and left. Later I took my chance to tell him, 'I am your eldest son. Not a nonentity, nor one of a crowd. Did you ever think of my feelings?' All he uttered was, 'Narayana … Narayana'.

It was unusual to see the house being cleaned up for the occasion. Ganesh was dusting the furniture. I smiled at him which he reciprocated with a significant look. Fifteen days ago I was sitting in the same small room when Bhimanna was brought from the toilet on a wheelchair. The heap of dust and rubbish had been removed now.

The numerous awards and honours received by Bhimanna jostled with each other for space on the shelves. Punyabhushan (Pride of Poona) and Maharashtra Bhushan (Pride of Maharashtra) were only a couple of them. The smaller ones were countless. There were some from the Hindi belt as well. A memento had also been given by the organizers of the Swami Haridas Sangeet Sammelan, where the swami is seen standing on the globe, perhaps crying secretly for an escape from such a sty. All awards were covered in a thick layer of dust and were bound together by a light network of cobwebs. I could almost hear their cries of protest!

Close to the door stood a shoe stand on which dried-up flowers lay bundled in a dried leaf roll around which ants played. It struck me that the leaf container also had prasad from the swami's math—the same prasad that Bhimanna held in such deep reverence and 'they' with such contempt. Even so, a group photograph published in *India Today* showed 'them' in the math with Bhimanna, all steeped in bhakti (deep devotion) of course. Lying around under the shoe stand were some unmatched footwear, perhaps waiting for their partner to be traced.

The next day the papers showed a photograph of the president, Bhimanna, and my stepsister's son. Limpets stick to great rocks and thereby lay claim to greatness. I sometimes think that if a man masters the art of being a good parasite, he will run short of nothing in life!

At about the same time the head of the Raghavendra Swami math of Mantralayam was on a visit to Poona. He wished to see Bhimanna and sent a messenger to find out of his availability. But the messenger was not admitted; in fact he was driven away. When Bhimanna came to know about the incident he called the local math, but the swami had already left for Chinchwad. Bhimanna regretted it sorely, but 'they' were totally insensitive to his feelings.

Dada Paranjpe, a senior professor of mathematics and a friend of Bhimanna's from Amravati, came to Poona to see his daughter. He wished to meet Bhimanna who had often stayed with him and his family. When he went to Bhimanna's house the guards at the gate asked him to come some other time. Dada lost his temper and raised his voice, which reached Bhimanna's ears and he asked his people to let Dada in.

Both of them then travelled down memory lane. As he was leaving, Bhimanna's prodigal tippler accosted Dada at the gate, 'So, the meeting is over. Was the feasting good?' Dada cast a cold glance at the parasite and left. He is said to have remarked later, 'These fellows have turned the father into an ATM'. This was like the priest controlling the god in the sanctum sanctorum. The list of such incidents can go on and on. The usual reaction from would-be visitors was, 'We put up with this because of our love and respect for Bhimanna.'

But NRIs and the affluent ones were always welcomed with studied smiles as they came with expensive gifts for Bhimanna.

He never forgot those who had helped and encouraged him during his apprentice years. Gratitude was his built-in virtue even after he became a celebrity. He secretly helped his old accompanists Shamacharya and Rotti Shinappa.

His cousin Narsu had often accompanied Bhimanna on the tanpura during his riyaz at Gadag. She did not receive even a shawl from him though expensive shawls were piled up on the stage after a concert in Hubli. The car boot used to be filled with coconuts, but she was never given even one. 'She' never allowed him to give away even such small things to his own people. He would then slam the door of the car boot to give vent to his anger.

Thakurdas, his accompanist on the harmonium, was suffering from throat cancer. Bhimanna wished to help him substantially, but he was not 'permitted' to do so. Dixit, who had expected Bhimanna to help Thakurdas, recounted this story to me.

Appa Jalgaonkar, another long-time harmonium accompanist, was brushed aside by 'her', although 'she' came from the same place as Appa's wife Dolly who knew of the skeletons in 'her' family's closet. 'She' cursed Appa saying 'You will die on the street'. However, he was a man of great dignity and was respected by all. He never spoke ill against Bhimanna. He knew the truth of the situation.

Dr Gokhale had been long associated with the Sawai Gandharva Sangeet Mahotsav and wanted to retire from his post of secretary. Once when he came to visit Bhimanna 'she' was heard shouting, 'Who is this Dr Gokhale? Is he a VIP?' Bhimanna pacified her in a suppressed tone and came out to meet Dr Gokhale. He was livid with anger and said to me, '*Who* is Dr Gokhale? He is the one who treated her in the dead of night when she had a stroke!' That was how people were treated after their help had been sought and given— the proverbial 'use-and-throw' policy.

In 1992 Bhimanna turned seventy. One day when I went to see him he was seated in a spacious chair and was chewing tobacco-paan. I touched his feet and sat down on a chair. I noticed others sitting there, and among them was the eminent vocalist Pandit Jasraj with his disciple Sanjeev Abhyankar, his wife, and their little daughter. Jasrajji looked dapper in his Assam silk dhoti and kurta. I felt embarrassed to see such luminaries sitting on the floor. I got up to sit down with them, but Bhimanna held my hand and signalled to me to not get up. I had no choice.

He did not go beyond 'Hmm....' The ball of tobacco in his mouth kept him mute. That was his way of refusing to speak. But, of course, he played with Sanjeev's daughter. The little one got up and planted a kiss on his cheek, which he liked immensely as evinced by his smile. Children were his weak point. Whenever he doffed his mask I always saw the face of an innocent child. Many took advantage of this to exploit him.

The visitors who came to meet Bhimanna knew well where the 'power centre' was and so they were sitting at the feet of the 'other woman'. After the visitors had left, he got up and spat out the tobacco from a window. 'Why did you keep mum?' I asked him. 'These people wish to organize an event in America to honour their guru. I am not willing to join. I have no mind to face all that hassle at my age now.' Nothing could ever shake his resolve.

When Bhimanna turned seventy-five, his fans decided to bring out a souvenir to mark the celebrations. Rambhau Kolhatkar asked me to contribute an article and sent someone to record my recollections. This was an unfamiliar mode for me and I spoke without reservation. When I came to talking about Mother, I got a little emotional and mentioned that Bhimanna had run away with 'her'. The story was floated around that his first wife (Mother) had been a mental case. I gave an old photograph of Bhimanna and asked for a copy of my recording.

The result was that the souvenir *Swaradhiraj* made no mention whatsoever of our family. On the other hand, 'her' family was highlighted as if they were of royal descent. I got a copy of the recording and was told that my narration had touched a sore point with them and had been deleted. Clearly this had been done on 'their' instructions and that, too, under the nose of Bhimanna himself. The organizers had no choice in the matter. I asked for two copies of the souvenir, one for Bhimanna's cousin Gopal and the other for me. Having received one copy I went through it and told Bhimanna not to send another. 'Why don't you want it now? Is it because it does not mention you all?' I held my tongue. After all he had full knowledge of the happenings. That was enough for my satisfaction.

As a mark of completing eighty years of life Sahasra Chandra Darshan (sighting of a thousand moons), a big yagna (holy fire), was performed at Bhimanna's house. 'When will you attend, in the morning or evening?' he asked me. He did not specify any time for us. We opted out as the invitation had been given casually. Though she was no more it was Mother's solemn and legitimate right to sit by Bhimanna's side in the ceremony. I went to see him after a couple of days. 'So, you did not attend? Give him the holy ashes,' he shouted, looking towards the drawing room. My stepsister came out to say that there were no ashes left. Bhimanna heaved a deep sigh and kept mum. That was how even ashes were denied to us. But I received a silver coin commemorating the event.

Bhimanna was selling his Opel, which the son of his friend wished to buy. The deal was settled and the car was to be paid for and picked up the following week. When he came to pick it up he found that the music system had been removed from the car. The young man looked inquiringly at Bhimanna, who whispered to him, 'Don't buy the car!' This incident throws a flood of light on the mentality of those people. Such were the devious ways of the people of the house!

Once a programme of bhakti sangeet (devotional songs) was organized to launch the heir apparent, with Bhimanna listening to it from a wheelchair in the wings. The singing was woefully out of tune and simply unbearable as some of the listeners in the audience told me over the phone. Even Bhimanna's charisma could not salvage the performance. It was an ingenious way of leveraging a disabled father (his body had already become a dilapidated museum of ailments). People felt fulfilled at the mere sight of him. Someone selling a pesticide as scent was rumoured to have achieved a marketing triumph in Europe. The said performance fell into that category. Subsequently, during the Sawai Gandharva Sangeet Mahotsav in 2008 Bhimanna's car was stationed at a corner of the stage during the 'young prince's' performance, with instructions to the compère to shower compliments on it. Bhimanna was lucky that his hearing ability had already weakened by then and the car windows had been rolled up and tightly shut because of the cold weather.

⚇

I was in Dharwad when my elder daughter-in-law Anita informed me that Bhimanna was going to be honoured with the Bharat Ratna. The previous day I had visited the ancient Shiva temple at Sirsi along with my wife, her cousin, and his wife. Looking at Shiva's Nandi (the bull), one got the feeling that Nandi was looking at Shiva with one eye and at Parvati with the other! While we were in the temple the electricity failed. The priest called out to me, 'Come forward, Nrusinhacharya!' I told him that my name was Raghavendra and that Narasimha was our family deity. 'Then do come forward,' he said. He opened the small gate of another temple on the precincts and led us through it. He stoked up the oil lamp and the full flame illuminated an image in front of us. It was not the usual image of Narasimha tearing open a demon's belly, but that of a sitting image. The priest pointed at the royal signet on the Lord's foot, then performed an arati. I was amazed to note that the face of the image bore a striking semblance to that of Bhimanna, so much so that it seemed as if he himself was sitting there! I wondered what inspiration had led the sculptor to carve such an image. For me it was an incredible coincidence.

At night all the TV channels flashed the news and I all but danced with joy. We—my wife and I, her cousin, and his

171

wife—started from Sirsi for Dharwad on a fine morning to visit Sudi, a beautiful place where Raghavendra Swami's guru Vadirajteerth used to live. This place was Bhimanna's favourite. The temple stood by the side of a lake. As we came out of the temple I happened to see two mongooses and a flock of *bharadwaj* (crow pheasant). This was an auspicious sign of the coming events, the great news!

After dinner I called Bhimanna in Poona. He had already had a loving word with my sons and daughters-in-law. He recognized my voice. I said, 'All this is by the grace of Raghavendra Swami, Guru, and your parents.' 'Absolutely,' he answered. 'Who else could give me so much?' I expressed my deep respect for him. Through the night a movie of the ups and downs in our lives flashed in my mind. Tears welled up in my eyes as I remembered Mother. How I wished she had been alive to see this day!

The next morning we—my wife and I—were mobbed by TV reporters. We gave our overjoyed reactions in Kannada. I was glad that I could speak fluently in Kannada.

On arriving in Poona I went to meet Bhimanna. The place was crowded with admirers. He smiled when he saw me, and I touched his feet with tear-flooded eyes. As I was bending over his feet, he stopped a celebrity from congratulating him. How immaturely people sometimes behave! The man seemed to have forgotten that, after all, Bhimanna was my father.

It was roses, roses all the way and everywhere in the place. I approached an acquaintance of mine who was sitting next to the 'other' family's son-in-law. My smile was returned with, 'All the riff-raff seem to be basking in the glory'. The taunt hurt me. This was like an inedible fruit claiming to have been nurtured by a mango tree! Once when Narayankaka had come to see Bhimanna, this same son-in-law was present. Bhimanna remarked to Narayankaka in a muffled voice, 'You are lucky. Your sons-in-law have their own homes. Look at this limpet here!' But, then, as I had met my god, I moved out of the place.

It was announced that government officials would visit Bhimanna at his home to confer the honour on him as he was not in a state to move. His fans were happy to have one more day of celebration as his birthday, too, was around the corner. When I went to his house a large crowd had already gathered there to greet him. Ganesh, the servant, was sending them away by telling that Bhimanna was not in. People placed their bouquets and left. The truth was that he was seriously ill. Ganesh tried to shoo me away, but I knew the truth and barged in.

I was accosted by 'her' elder daughter-in-law (whom Bhimanna referred to as 'deputy'). 'We aren't allowing anyone to see him today,' she said. 'I will not leave without seeing him,' I replied sharply. 'Wait then,' she rasped. I saw his disciple Upendra Bhat moving around. All else was quiet. 'Her' younger son approached me and said, 'You met him a couple of days ago. Why do you wish to see him again?' 'Who are you to decide when I am to meet him? You stand at number seven, remember that!' I replied nonchalantly. He understood well enough that I was senior to him by twenty-two years and, hence, his elder. But he seemed to be in a belligerent mood and challenged me, 'What can you do?' In fact, he tried to grapple with me. I restrained myself and said, 'I am no longer young enough to indulge in such things. I want to see Bhimanna for a minute and I will leave. You, too, can be present.' The door of Bhimanna's room was opened and I entered.

Bhimanna lay moaning with pain. His body had turned very dark. He was clearly not in a good state of health. Even so I had to tell him what had happened. 'Your younger son tried to manhandle me,' I said in Kannada. 'Who?' he asked, in a pain-filled voice. 'Your pampered one. He's not worthy of even having his name mentioned,' I said. He understood and moaned, '*Ayyayyo ... ayyayyo....*' 'I have repeatedly told you that I will be present when the Bharat Ratna is conferred on you. I will bear all expenses, regardless of where it is held. Inform the organizers accordingly.' 'Yes, I will,' he said. I left after touching his feet. The despicable creature was not to be seen anywhere around. As a matter of fact I could have settled the bout there and then itself. However, with such a great event being just two days away, I did not wish to raise any dust. I called Bhimanna in the evening again to remind him of my wish. 'Yes, I have already informed them. Come over,' he said affectionately.

I had always wished for a Bharat Ratna for Bhimanna. And now it was to become a reality. When I mentioned it to him he said, 'I don't feel any excitement now'. He was the darling of thousands of music lovers. His place was in their hearts. He wanted nothing more in life. Even then the formalities had to be observed. The day dawned. I performed a puja and went to his house. Crowds had already gathered at his gate and the place had been cordoned off by the police. However, I was allowed entry as many of them seemed to know me. There were reporters and TV people milling around. No seating arrangements had been made. Only government-deployed cameramen were allowed in. It was a sad scene inside: beautiful images of the saints Dnyaneshwar and Ganapati stood at the entrance and a heap of footwear lay near them. It was heartbreaking to see them disrespected like that, and I started to pick up the footwear to put it to one side when a police officer came running and said, 'No, no. Don't do it yourself.

I'll get it done.' 'Also put some flowers on the images,' I suggested and went in.

The heir apparent was ready, fully made-up, talking to the cameramen. 'He, too, will want a CD,' he told them pointing at me. This was an unbelievable contrast with the way he had behaved towards me only two days ago. The small room was crowded with 'her' sisters, the heir apparent's friend, Bhimanna's disciple, the media father (advisor to the 'other' family), and government officials. 'Her' framed photograph hung just above a portrait of Raghavendra Swami's made by Mr Pandit. The juxtaposition was inappropriate and I asked the heir apparent to remove it. 'I haven't put it there,' he said and turned away. Many beautiful bouquets lay outside, but no one had bothered to arrange them to make a good background.

I had an intense desire to be a witness to the ceremony and felt that I was in seventh heaven. Hundreds of his performances flashed before my eyes. 'Her' sisters and servants had already commandeered the seats just behind Bhimanna's chair: everyone wanted to be seen with him. I sat down on the mattress on the floor at the feet of Bhimanna's chair.

Bhimanna entered the room, helped by someone. He looked fit at least for the event, although he had been quite unwell a couple of days ago. He looked at me and asked, 'How was it today?' 'Joy all the way,' I answered. The context was the earlier rough handling incident, but nobody understood this.

After he sat down, the official representing the president came forward and said, 'As per instructions from the president I confer on you this honour of Bharat Ratna'. He held the certificate before Bhimanna. Then he took out the gold, peepul-leaf-shaped medallion and held it in front of Bhimanna. 'This is, now, your possession. Kindly put it on,' he suggested. At this, the elder son got up and, balancing himself, put the medal around Bhimanna's neck. This man was known to all Poona. The precious pendant in his hands seemed sacrilegious. I felt that the Rashtrapati's representative ought to have put it around Bhimanna's neck. A round of claps followed and it was all virtually over.

Asked to give his response Bhimanna said in English, 'I am grateful and thankful to the honourable Rashtrapatiji and to the people of India'. When he learnt that the officials were from Bihar, he inquired about a member of a royal family from there. All this while the younger son was trying to whisper in Bhimanna's ears. Harshavardhan Patil sat next to Bhimanna. His son-in-law, the heir apparent, and Dr Atul Joshi sat on the other side. When Bhimanna tried to speak a little more he was restrained. Samosas and sweets were served on paper plates. I touched Bhimanna's feet and told him in Kannada that I wished to be photographed with him. The 'others' watched me derisively and frowned, but Bhimanna agreed. I stood behind him, put my hands on his shoulders and we were quickly photographed.

It had been announced that Bhimanna wished to have a simple ceremony. The fact was that the world was not to know how seriously weak Bhimanna had become after his illness, both in body and in mind. The photographers had been strictly instructed that only those pictures approved by the 'other' family should be published.

I have no words to express my elation. India's highest civilian honour had been conferred on my father. It was the first of its kind for Hindustani vocal classical music. My mind was filled with memories of Mother, of Bhimanna's parents, and of Raghavendra Swami. Before Bhimanna could speak to the press he was whisked away, and within twenty minutes or so the entire ceremony was over.

The chairs arranged for President Kalam's visit still stood in the veranda, gathering dust. The minister, the officers, and the reporters had to sit on them; some of them had to sit down on the floor. It was a striking example of mismanagement. No one seemed to take seriously such a momentous event.

Although I was Bhimanna's eldest son, no reporter except one TV man had bothered to seek my response. I said, 'He was very happy today. This is a highly blessed day in our life.' I also said to another one, 'I felt as though I were in the sanctum sanctorum of Lord Pandurang, watching the puja from close up'.

Soon all doors of the house were shut tight and servants were asked to guard them. All the members of 'that' family had disappeared. I soon realized why there was so much secrecy: the officials of the central government had brought a cheque as a part of the honour, and I was not to get a whiff of it. Small-mindedness never leaves some people even at such great moments. Whenever Bhimanna sang Bhairavi I used to feel that my life should come to an end with those notes. But people do have different reasons for their existence.

Eventually, after repeated requests, I did get a few photographs from the official photographer. The promised CD, however, never came my way, though Bhimanna was a witness to my request for the same. Sufficient care was taken to release pictures to newspapers showing only 'that' family.

Couldn't it have been done differently, with due dignity and propriety, for the thousands of people—the audiences, the critics, the fellow artists—who had showered so much love on Bhimanna? It could have been held in a public hall where a car could have easily taken him for the ceremony. Even some of his disciples had been denied entry to his house. Not even recorded shehnai music had been played. The entire arrangement displayed crass poverty of imagination and goodwill.

Only 'her' sisters and relatives had been present. It was 'they' who had raised a protective wall around 'her' when 'she' ran away with Bhimanna from Badami. Sometimes even the lion withdraws when faced with a pack of hyenas that try to snatch away its food. That was what had happened to Bhimanna.

I felt sorely unhappy that the city of Poona, where Bhimanna lived, flourished, and was honoured so generously, had been deprived of sharing in the glory and glamour of the momentous honour of the Bharat Ratna for him. A short but memorable celebration could have been arranged. What had happened was a closed formality open only to a few gatecrashers and 'that family's' attendants. The most perturbing fact was the total indifference of the media to such a mediocre management.

~

1.   James Beverage, a Canadian industrialist, has made a documentary titled *Miyamalhar* on Bhimanna.

Twelve

THE CONFERRING OF THE BHARAT RATNA was followed by countless interviews and articles in the media. Those who knew me also were aware of my passionate admiration for Bhimanna. One such acquaintance came to see me with a request to recount my reminiscences of him. I spoke non-stop for two hours. 'Your reminiscences are valuable as they shed a lot of light on the real Bhimanna. Take it from me that I will surely interview you for TV,' he said as he left.

This made me very conscious of a new responsibility—that of writing my memories. No other thoughts filled my mind for the next eight days and I began to write several hours a day at a stretch. On the date for the TV interview I was told that one more artist would also be interviewed, but I was not to disclose my identity to him. He had been informed that I was to be interviewed for some other topic than his. All this precaution had to be exercised because he belonged to the 'other' camp and had he known about the topic of my interview, the 'others' would surely have done everything possible to forestall it.

My two-episode interview on ETV Marathi attracted a lot of attention, and the telephone calls complimenting me did not stop. Despite this being my very first appearance on television media, I had fielded the questions with confidence, and without a single retake. I concluded the interview by singing some lines of the bhajan 'Teerth Vitthal, kshetra Vitthal' popularized by Bhimanna. I had, as it were, merged my entire being with Bhimanna's, and when I opened my eyes after singing, I saw the producer and the cameraman bowing before me with respect. Clearly this was in obeisance to Bhimanna's notes. Soon after the interview was telecast the producer received a threatening call, 'Why did you invite him? My accountant [he meant "advocate"] will now take care of you!' The producer responded coolly, 'Do whatever you want'. My article 'My Father, Bhimanna', published in the magazine *Antarnaad*, also evoked excellent response. I had written there, 'Bhimanna's music is a combination of willpower, a lofty imagination, and notes immersed in emotion'.

Soon after a media friend of the 'other' camp telecast a programme titled *Nakshatranche Dene* (A Gift from the Stars) on Zee TV. Viewers were flabbergasted to watch it; Bhimanna's students were dressed like members of a brass band. Earlier the same programme had been presented at the Bal Gandharva Rang Mandir in Poona. When I tried to book a ticket I was denied it. I explained who I was. This evoked some whispering at the other end of the line, and finally I was given a clear 'No'. This was, of course, the usual expression of small-mindedness.

The performance at Bal Gandharva was a disappointment. It was also telecast, beginning with Bhimanna's well-known *'Yeri maayi aaj shubh mangal gaao'* (Sing something sacred), but the faces wore expressions of sadness. Only the producer became sad thereafter due to adverse feedback. But the 'cat' had got away with more than its share of butter. Vocalists like Shankar Mahadevan and Arati Ankalikar had performed in the event, but without any spark of Bhimanna's music. I thought of calling it 'star curse' instead of 'star gift'. The producer confessed that he had failed to assess correctly the talent of the performers.

A special function presided over by the vocalist Gangubai Hangal was organized in Hubli to celebrate the honour conferred on Bhimanna. My brother Anand sang a few bhajans popularized by Bhimanna and I recounted some of my reminiscences in Kannada. Gangubai was so moved that she held my hand tightly throughout the speech.

When Bhimanna's health was slightly improved my wife and I toured Kerala for a week or so after which I paid him a visit. The conversation that followed was highly interesting and, hence, is reproduced here. My interview on ETV had touched a sore point of the 'other' people. I had said in it that eight years after marriage and after fathering three children Bhimanna had eloped from Badami with a girl who had come to him as a disciple. This had clearly exposed the illegitimate status of 'her' and her children. When I bent to touch his feet Bhimanna said in Kannada, 'Raghu, I learn that you have told lies in your TV interview'. (I could instantly see that this nonsense had been stuffed into his head by them.) Undisturbed I asked him, 'Did you watch it?'

'No'.

'Then how can you say this? Were you not down with typhoid in Badami?'

'Yes, it was so.'

'Did you not go to Nagpur?'

'Yes, I did.'

'Then where is the falsehood? I am your son and related a few of my reminiscences about you, and I also sang a few lines. Nothing inappropriate was uttered. Your students Ramkrishna Patwardhan and Narayan Deshpande praised me for it. As for falsehood, what about the crass lies told by those children of yours in the book *Bhimsen*? Shamakka had remarked, "Who'll marry this tanpura fellow?" What those people got into print was that Mother did not wish to marry you!'

Bhimanna's only reaction to this was to start humming some notes. This was his way of putting a full stop to any topic. He never mentioned it thereafter. I wish he had seen that interview. It would have shown him how totally immersed I was in my devotion to him and his music, and that I was an inseparable part of him. But, of course, he was well aware of it.

E-Sakal interviewed me at my bungalow, Bageshree, at Dhayari and uploaded it on YouTube. Within eight minutes I painted a beautiful image of Bhimanna. Thousands all over the world viewed it, and it is viewed even today.

I spoke for two hours on 'Bhimanna, As I Understand Him' in Barrister Nath Pai's *Vyakhyanmala* series in Belgaum and threw a flood of light on Bhimanna's personality.

In his book *Bhimsen*, Potdar mentions his several visits abroad. I am a witness to the harsh words he had hurled at Mother—his legitimately wedded wife and mother of his four children—who had asked for money for her pilgrimage to Badri–Kedar for which I bore part of the expenses. My maternal aunt Premakka and her husband Hungund accompanied her on the pilgrimage. Those were a few moments of happiness in her life.

While in the USA Bhimanna had stayed with Prabhakar Rao, who managed all his expenses. Every time Bhimanna would ask him to buy things in pairs. 'He always seemed under some tension. Subsequently I learnt that one of the pair was for his first wife,' he told me later. I explained to him what the real story was, for we received absolutely nothing after his trips. 'She' must have seen to it that nothing reached us, regardless of what Bhimanna may have wished for.

Bhimanna was great. He was kind. Even so I have seen him in his most ruthless moods with Mother, obviously due to the poison 'she' injected into his heart. The melodious maestro on such occasions was totally out of tune for us. Those used to be excruciating moments for us. Maybe he was trying to pacify 'her' tantrums for his own peace of mind. We used to feel singed in the fires of his temper. Valmiki, who wrote the Ramayana, too, was held responsible by his own people for the sins he had committed for those same people. 'She' and later 'her' children always claimed that Bhimanna belonged to them only. Fie on the hypocritical world with its 'holier than thou' attitude which turns a blind eye to such lies!

I have seen some of 'them' crossing, wearing chappals, over Bhimanna's dead body covered with an old piece of cloth in a room. What misfortune for such a great one!

At Dhayari we used to buy milk from our neighbour Pandit Mahadevshastri Joshi. It was always a great joy to talk with his wife Sudhatai, while his words were like precious gems for us. Several writers often visited him and I happened to be present on one such occasion. Panditji introduced me to them with the words, 'He is Bhimsen Joshi's son. But he shines with his own light.' He was a witness to our hard life, as my wife and I used to be away from home during the day at our respective workplaces. When not working I would be busy with the plants and trees in my garden. Since we were not in a position to stay close to Bhimanna's residence, he would occasionally drop in at ours. Instead of clinging to him like a parasite, I preferred to be linked to his music. This has stayed permanently with me. Even when I was working deep in a well, while the drilling machine was biting into the earth and the compressor was whirring, I would be crooning his notes in my head.

Insanity and greatness are conjoined in an artist's life. The world often looks upon them as mad people. I, too, inherited this streak from Bhimanna. Once when I met him at Raghavendra Swami's math, I asked him whether he would take me as an accompanist on the tanpura. He smiled sadly and said, 'I'll think about it'. Obviously he knew that 'she' would violently oppose it. He would often tell me, 'It is a matter of great luck to get a good guru'. I, too, could not have accepted anyone but Bhimanna as my guru. Whenever I was asked why I did not train myself in vocal music, I often quoted the poet Kusumagraj's lines from his immortal poem *'Pruthviche Premgeet'* (Love Song of the Earth):

How long will you deceive me, O sun?
Millennia on end?
How long am I to circle within your orbit
Begging for your love?
But better be far away
Than a union of the weak![1]

Nevertheless the fact remains that I had listened to Bhimanna's riyaz that would stretch for eight hours. The music had sunk into my very being and I have continued to enjoy it every minute of my life. Music, like Ayurveda, is a way of life. You are in harmony with the world if you are in tune with yourself. Harmony becomes a way of life for you. Life brings both sorrow and happiness. Even the gods are not an exception to this law of life. Who am I to be an exception to it?

I have faced several moments of extreme dejection and suffering in life. I came out of them with the help of music and faith. One of Bhimanna's Kannada bhajans, *'Na ninna dhyanalu iralu sada, mik manavarenu madavru?'* (God, I am always in meditation of you, how can evil forces harm me?) provided me succour. His music spelt bliss and fulfilment for me. Whenever I felt hurt by his indifference to us, it was, again, his music that lifted me up from the deep morass. I lived like Ashwathhama of the Mahabharata who had to bear his wounds for life. But he had killed Draupadi's children. Whose blood did I have on my hands? The burning desire to get Bhimanna's 'musical' blessings died a slow death. I have experienced the pangs of those who have suffered humiliation and rejection for generations together without their fault. They had a Bharat Ratna father in Dr Ambedkar; I too had one!

I met an old gentleman, Mr Prabhu, at a friend's house in Poona. He had taken some lessons in music from Devdhar, a well-known teacher, and was the general manager of a factory in Bhopal. Prabhu asked me to sing raga Marwa and I sang for half an hour. Tears glistened in his eyes. 'People practise for fifty years and do not reach where you are now. Alas! A whole banquet is laid before you but you are not allowed to eat ...' he said.

I attended hundreds of Bhimanna's concerts. Initially they used to be moderate in-house performances. One such concert was arranged in Raste Wada where personalities like Sardar Abasaheb Mujumdar, Dattopant Deshpande, and Dr Nanasaheb Deshpande sat in the audience. Bhimanna started with raga Yaman with an hour-long exposition. They were moments when the listeners were so immersed that they forgot their selves. Every improvisation of taan fell like a heavenly shower on them and gave rise to many a 'Wah-wah!' and 'Kya baat hai!' (What a fantastic expression!). Appreciation from Abasaheb was the ultimate recognition for artists in those days.

Then followed the natya sangeet 'Chandrika hee janu' (She is moon incarnate). Bhimanna couched it in the Carnatic style almost for half an hour. And then came the spellbinding *'Aur nahin kachhu kaam'* (There is no other wish) in raga Darbari. The audience were stunned by the skill, reflection, and intellectual flash of the renditions. The recital culminated in the immortal poetry of *'Jhanak jhanak waa more bichwaa'* (My bangles jingle). Finally at the request of the entire audience, he presented raga Bhairavi taught to him by his guru Sawai Gandharva. Some of those present in the audience had heard the guru.

I listened to Bhimanna umpteen times at the Lakshmi Krida Mandir auditorium in Poona. Morning performances invoked the appropriate ragas like Lalit, Todi, Jogiya, Komal Rishabh Asavari, and Ramkali, while Marwa, Multani, Puriya Dhanashree, Chhayanat, Durga, and Bihag were presented during evening concerts. He moved like a monarch among them. The audience used to be thrilled by his *'Baiya badarwa barasat aaye'* (The clouds have come down pouring) in raga Surdasi Malhar. Sometimes the legendary Bal Gandharva himself would attend these performances. Whenever he came Bhimanna would get up, put a garland around him, and lie flat in reverence at his feet. The entire hall would be spellbound at the sight.

Bhimanna was always a darling of classical-music lovers and no Ganapati festival in Poona, or elsewhere, could be complete without his concerts. People jostled for space on such occasions and whoever stopped out of curiosity to see what was happening was sure to be glued to his spot till the very end. His music was like a spider's web in which one gets caught and feels lost.

He was once felicitated in a city square along with a wrestler, who was honoured with the Maharashtra Kesari title. Both of them fell to discussing different tricks in wrestling, for Bhimanna had trained himself in that sport in Jalandhar. However, when Bhimanna's concert started, the wrestler saluted and said, 'This quite beats me ... it's beyond me....'

Bhimanna often performed in the Nad Habba festival of the Karnataka Association. On such occasions he would wear a dhoti and kurta, and looked dapper in the outfit. Sometimes he would sit in the *veerasana* pose while singing demanding notes. While singing the lower notes he would bend down almost touching the seat, giving the effect of a sonorous rumbling of clouds. That was his lung power.

I remember in particular his performance during a Nad Habba festival at Daund, a railway colony south of Poona, which I had attended. It was arranged in a small but presentable hall with a tiled compound wall. Akashmogra trees, loaded with white flowers, some of which had covered the roots of the trees, lined the sides of the plot. It was a moonlit night. Bhimanna's very first upper note held out a promise of a rare performance. He began with Shuddh Kalyan; then came the thumri '*Nadiya kinare mora gaon*' (My village is located by a riverside) in raga Pilu. He laced it with a Punjabi flavour, thrilling the audience who responded with many an 'Encore'. And after the interval came a Kannada bhajan '*Bhagyada Lakshmi Baramma*' (Goddess Lakshmi, giver of fortune, come to my place and bless me).

Then he commenced with the second half of the concert with a fresh smile on his face. He cast a glance at me and began raga Malkauns. I had whispered to him during the interval that Malkauns would be most welcome. He regaled the audience with it for two hours. It was as if he had raised a Taj Mahal with his notes. The main verse '*Rangraliya karat sautan ke sang*' (Enjoying the company of the other woman) was a feast for the ears. He concluded with the popular bhajan

'*Jo bhaje Hari ko sada*' (One who always worships Hari will attain ultimate bliss) in raga Bhairavi.

The dinner that followed was a delicious treat with jowar bhakri, chilli chutney, curds, and a green salad—all favourites of Bhimanna's. I sat with him in the train compartment on the return journey, but all the way I felt like Wordsworth after he had heard the Solitary Reaper's song: 'The music in my heart I bore/ Long after it was heard no more.'

A foreign delegation was visiting Poona and a special performance of Bhimanna was arranged. An admirer, Raghunathrao Limaye, had organized a private concert. Raghunathrao was close to Abdul Karim Khan Sahib and Sawai Gandharva. Bhimanna insisted that Vitthalrao Sardeshmukh should accompany him on the harmonium. Vitthalrao agreed on the condition that he would not have to speak with Bhimanna! When Raghunathrao mentioned it to Bhimanna his response was, 'He will, after he listens to me!'

It was a select audience and the whole atmosphere was charged with joy. Bhimanna began with raga Puriya and concluded the five-hour concert with raga Bhairavi. Vitthalrao Sardeshmukh could not resist himself and warmly embraced Bhimanna, tears flowing from his eyes. The legend goes that the great vocalist Miyan Tansen of Emperor Akbar's court could melt a stone with his singing. Bhimanna, too, had the same impact on the hearts of his listeners. Bal Dandekar, who was in the audience, told me that the performance was unforgettable.

The three-day celebration of the Sawai Gandharva Sangeet Mahotsav used to be an unending feast for music lovers. Bhimanna's rendering of raga Jogiya, which I had heard then, had transported me into a magical world. I felt as though I were being led by someone through a garden in full bloom.

I could almost smell the fragrance. I had a similar experience while listening to sitar maestro Vilayat Khan's performance. Bhimanna used to perform on the last day of the festival. I would see him in the green room where he practised. It was a unique experience to listen to him informally. His dedication to his guru gave his music a heavenly touch. The festival customarily concluded with a recorded performance of Sawai Gandharva's *'Bin dekhe par naahi chain'* (I have no comfort without seeing the beloved) in raga Bhairavi. A pensive stillness would fill the atmosphere for some time after such a performance.

Once when I entered the green room on the occasion of a Sawai Gandharva Sangeet Mahotsav, I saw Bhimanna lying on the ground. He had washed and dressed for the performance. He had not slept for two nights and, therefore, was resting for a while with his eyes closed. I could see the holy ashes on his forehead. Two students were tuning the tanpuras and another was pressing Bhimanna's feet. I, too, started giving him a massage. The moment I touched him he asked, 'Is that Raghu?' I said, 'Yes, Bhimanna,' and a wave of extreme happiness ran down my spine!

The organizers were tense by this time. Bhimanna's friend Dixit said, 'Anna, Feroze Dastur is performing on stage. It is the last but one item and then you have to take over.' At that very moment Bhimanna got up, gulped down a cup of tea, instructed his students to start singing, and he himself lay down and started snoring!

Full of anxiety, Dixit wondered how the exhausted Bhimanna could perform. Another cup of tea was sent for him. The students started singing. Again Dixit coaxed Bhimanna to get up. Eventually he opened his eyes wide, gulped down some more tea, and the first solid note emerged from his throat. Relief and happiness filled the hearts of those present in the dressing room. He began 'Change nayanwa' in raga Todi and the room was filled a soft, silvery mist of musical notes.

To recall such memories is to open a sack full of pearls. Every pearl brings the same joy of recognition.

However, the thorn of one Sawai Gandharva Sangeet Mahotsav has dug deep into my memory. When Bhimanna completed sixty years, the Arya Sangeet Prasarak Mandal organized a public felicitation at Renuka Swaroop Memorial Girls High School. He was honoured with the customary garland, a shawl, and a coconut. The 'other' woman was also traditionally honoured with sari and kumkum on the forehead. Mother sat in the audience and I saw tears flowing down her cheeks. She was the one who had the right to sit by Bhimanna for such honours. I, too, felt like someone had thrown a bucket of cold water on me.

I overheard some women commenting on Mother's simple outfit. How insensitive of them! Would the mother of three who had been abandoned by her husband dress like a model on the ramp with a studied smile on her lips? How would those loose-tongued women have dressed if a similar fate had befallen them? And shouldn't the organizers have honoured Mother with a simple gesture of putting the kumkum on her forehead and giving her a shawl? Mother often said, 'My own money is counterfeit. Why blame the world? You should do no wrong. If you try to crush the scorpion sitting on God's head, you will only end up hitting God!' How twisted are the ways of the world!

But, at least, one member of the organization wrote a letter of condolence when Mother passed away. The vocal maestro Gangubai Hangal wrote, *Your mother was made of steel. Her*

forbearance knew no bounds. It was she who had stood firmly by
Bhimanna when he was searching for his way in life. It was her
single-minded support that eventually helped Bhimanna to rise. May
her soul rest in peace.

When 'she' died her relatives instituted a prize for classical singing from the funds of the Sawai reservoir. This was like blowing one's own trumpet. It was robbing Paul to pay Peter. What an insatiable greed for fame! Stalwarts like vocalists Hirabai Barodekar, Feroze Dastur, Gangubai Hangal, and Dr Nanasaheb Deshpande were among the trustees, but none of them had ever fallen prey to such cheap behaviour. In the course of time sycophants had inveigled their way into the trust and thrived on its funds. Some of them even chose to become mere reservation clerks who could siphon off their own share of the profits. The festival was renamed Sawai Gandharva Bhimsen Sangeet Mahotsav, thus placing the disciple above the guru. Bhimanna himself would have hardly tolerated such sacrilege. Clearly the trust was on its way to becoming a permanent source for feeding parasites.

Bhimanna had a wide company of great contemporaries like Kumar Gandharva, Vasantrao Deshpande, Amir Khan, Mallikarjun Mansoor, Sangameshwar Gurav, Pandit Jasraj, Pandit Jitendra Abhisheki, Kesarbai Kerkar, and Gangubai Hangal, among others. The Kirana Gharana also boasted of many good disciples among whom there existed a keen but healthy competition, but the rules of decency were never trespassed. Harmony ruled all relationships. Mutual respect was a way of life. I have seen Bhimanna bowing in respect before senior artists.

In those days it was difficult for artists to make two ends meet. It would have been nothing short of *harakiri* (suicide) if I had followed a career in vocal music. One could survive only if the family coffers were full. One had to be the best if one wished to depend solely on a career in arts. Most of them chose to be teachers or tried to find a job in radio. Among Bhimanna's students Ramkrishna Patwardhan worked in the postal service, Narayan Deshpande was employed in Burmah-Shell, Shreepati Padigar owned a restaurant, Upendra Bhat worked in New India Assurance Corporation, and Madhav Gudi lived with Bhimanna and always accompanied him on tanpura. But he, too, was hard up and did not own a house. Artists could not survive on art alone.

Nowadays even second-grade performers make good money. Some of them may earn a good livelihood merely by playing the tanpura and repeating 'Yes, sir', 'No, sir'. Unfortunately, Bhimanna's students could not make the mark. They remained tethered to the ground, their singing was largely devoid of emotion, their lung power was weak. Bhimanna would shout, 'Are you on an empty stomach today?' while he continued to perform vigorously till his late seventies! Who would wish to listen to a substitute Bhimanna as long as the original still commanded the stage?

Today we live in an age of 'managing' everything; there are no limits to showmanship. Singers display their material ornaments on stage, but the real ornament—that of talent—remains covered; perhaps, it is absent. (But, of course, there are exceptions.) Rave reviews can be managed; paid news is common. One sees only rats when lions are expected. It is far more rewarding to listen at home to the recorded concerts of greats like Bhimsen, Amir Khan, Kishori Amonkar, Prabha Atre, Kumar Gandharva, Pandit Jasraj, Pandit Jitendra Abhisheki, and such gifted ones. Maestros like Bhimsen used to enter the heart and soul of a raga through deep meditation on it. Bhimsen would dive deep into a raga and open up a whole new universe before his audience. One could not tell the singer from the song; 'How can we know the dancer from the dance?' as Yeats had remarked.

Bhimanna added a fourth dimension to his music with his untiring efforts, riyaz, and commitment. No wonder his notes resonated with the chords of his audience's hearts. His body language itself was expressive of the moods of the various ragas. It was like butterflies flitting around flowers. One could almost smell the fragrance.

Bhimanna once gave an exclusive and extremely memorable performance of natya sangeet at Abasaheb Garware College in Poona. Several stage artists and singers were also present. The traditional *naandi* (the prologue) created a rainbow of unforgettable notes. The favourite Kannada bhajan 'Bhagyada Lakshmi Baramma' followed after the intermission. Although I had listened to it many times before, this turned out to be an entirely unique and dazzling performance. It was as if both the goddesses—Saraswati the goddess of wisdom and Lakshmi the goddess of wealth—were dancing to the notes!

Eminent connoisseurs sat in the audience, their cheeks moist with tears.

I know many learned critics of classical music. I often feel that they have blunted sensibilities. They fail to understand the importance of emotion expressed in music. They also fail to understand the subterranean fourth dimension of Bhimanna's singing. They would regard it as a mere tour de force, a feat of strength or skill. But, then, they also think that Bhimanna is class apart. Clearly enough, these critics are well versed in the grammar of the art, but they somehow fail to fathom the soul. This reminds me of Bhimanna's bhajan '*Jhoote jag mein dil lalcha kar asal watan kyo chhod diya? Naam japan kyo chhod diya?*' (Why are you deluded by the specious and give up the genuine? Why have you given up chanting God's name?).

After all, the quantity of water you can carry from the Ganges depends on your container! The same is true of imbibing music at the feet of a maestro.

Bhimanna's special programmes of santwani opened up a new vista in semi-classical music. His guru, too, used to perform special bhajans, which attracted admirers from far and wide. Bhimanna had learnt bhajans from his mother. He had grown up with the chanting of mantras and prayers said by his father every morning. They had seeped into his very being. As a result whenever he sang bhajans, his being transformed into that of a saint; he was, as it were, devotion incarnate. He took his audiences on a pilgrimage of communion with God. His various renditions of the slow-paced bhajan *'Jai jai Rama Krishna Hari'* (Victory to Rama, Krishna, Hari) would send the devotees of Lord Vitthal at Pandharpur into a dancing frenzy. *'Pandhari-nowasa sakhya Panduranga/ kari ang-sanga bhaktanchiya'* (O my friend Panduranga [Vitthala], who lives at Pandharpur, please embrace your devotees), *'Roop pahata lochani/ Sukh jhale wo sajani'* (When I see God's beautiful face, I get supreme bliss), *'Anuraniya thokada, Tuka akasha evhdha'* (Says Tuka, I am tinier than an atom and greater than the sky), and the Kannada bhajan *'Sriniketana palayamam'* (O God Vishnu, bless me and take care of me) were always hits. He knew a hundred ways of singing 'Teerth Vitthal, kshetra Vitthal'. It was as if Lord Vitthal himself were present on the stage. His thousand ways of pronouncing 'Vitthal' indeed showed the thousand avatars of the Lord. He would usually conclude with *'Aga Vaikunthichya raya/ Raya Vitthal sakhaya'* (O King of Vaikunth, you are my beloved friend) in raga Bhairavi.

His popularity as a bhajan singer had no parallels. His lasting contribution is in the form of elevating the lyrical bhajan form to the dignity of classical concerts. It was a garland offered by him to Lord Vitthal. His Kannada bhajans have become a part of Vitthal worship in the Marathi-speaking world as well.

Bhimanna was, indeed, lucky to get composers like Shrinivas Khale and Ram Phatak for *santwaniabhanga*s (bhajans by Marathi, Kannada, and Sanskrit saints). He gave thousands of performances of the programme. I have seen many people from the audience coming up to touch Bhimanna's feet after the performance. Once I, too, wished to greet him and so I went to the green room. There I saw those 'merchants of art' greedily counting wads of currency notes, which they put away as soon as I approached. The programme was made available on recorded discs which sold in lakhs. They are played by the varkaris on their pilgrimage to Vithoba's temple at Pandharpur. I can see that as long as these devotees go on this pilgrimage Bhimanna's santwani will continue to be played. These abhangas are sung in even the far-flung villages of Karnataka.

Bhimanna's Kannada bhajans by Purandara Dasa are equally popular. He learnt them at his mother's feet. He would go back to his childhood whenever he sang them. They were like mother's milk for him. 'Bhagyada Lakshmi Baramma' has become an all-time favourite of Kannadigas, and the bhajans are played at special pujas during Diwali. His Sanskrit bhajans rendered for the Vaishno Devi Trust like '*Namo namami mata bhagavati*' (I salute the Goddess), '*Prapannaadi hare praseed*' (O Goddess of intelligence, bless me and give me your holy blessing of talent), and '*Ya devi sarva bhuteshu*' (One who is a Goddess to all the living beings) evoke the divine atmosphere of the Himalayas and are a rare cultural treasure today. The Sanskrit words uttered by him fall like dewdrops of God's grace on the mind.

His Hindi bhajans by saints like Kabir and Brahmanand are equally popular. '*Be tan mundane be mundane*' (All the time decorating your body [which will go to the earth one day]), '*Bhajman Rama charan sukhdai*' (O my mind, worship the sacred and happiness-giving feet of Rama), '*Prabhu kar sab dukh door hamare*' (O God, remove all our suffering), 'Sab paise ke bhai', and '*Jo bhaje Hari ko sada*' (One who worships Hari for ever) are like nectar falling on the souls of the audience.

His bhajans took Bhimanna to the very roots of India's commoners, in whose hearts he carved a niche for himself. My uncle once told me that Bhimanna had run away to Pandharpur when he was barely nine years old. He went to Guru Warkhedi there who had taught Sanskrit to Bhimanna's father. He loved Bhimanna, looked after him for a couple of weeks, bought him new clothes, and took him back to his father in Gadag. During his stay in Pandharpur, Bhimanna used to accompany the guru into the sanctum sanctorum of Vithoba's temple. I believe this holy covenant with Lord Vitthal eventually inspired Bhimanna to render the santwani bhajans!

~

1. From 'Love Song of the Earth', a well-known poem by the Marathi poet Kusumagraj.

Thirteen

EARLIER IN HIS CAREER Bhimanna used to accept invitations to perform in public places where the common people would have a chance to listen to a celebrity. He was able to pull in crowds there as well because the taste for classical music transcends class boundaries. He would often chat with pedestrians whenever he walked the lanes and by lanes of the city. He used to attend the eminent procession of Ganapati in Poona on immersion day. People would see him praying to Ganapati in the public square of the Bhanuvilas Theatre. He personally knew several office-bearers of public organizations and, as a result, invitations to perform used to come in every year.

He knew that it was good for celebrated artists to keep in contact with the ordinary people. He never showed a sense of superiority in his interaction with them. I have met artists who show scant consideration towards their admirers. Such people have no place in society; they should live in the Himalayas. They feel that now that Bhimanna is no more they are Bharat Ratna awardees! I have decided not to attend their performances.

Bhimanna lived with a sense of guilt, whether with the knowledge of having done injustice to us—a permanent pinch of conscience—or because of harassment by the people around him. Hounded by these ghouls he even tried to commit suicide once. When this failed he started to drink heavily.

However, in the course of time he successfully de-addicted himself though there were 'some' who claimed credit for it. There were hacks to cajole such people.

In 1983 Shankar Abhyankar, who used to deliver spiritual discourses, wrote Bhimanna's biography, *Swar-Bhaskar*.[1] It is a good and true account of Bhimanna's life, and has a much higher literary value than Potdar's *Bhimsen*, whose knowledge of classical music is suspect. Potdar has admitted this in the preface to his book. His friends told me that he was frustrated because he had not been allowed to write a truthful account of Bhimanna's life. It often reads like a rehash of the earlier publication *Swar-Bhaskar*.

By the time I came to the concluding pages of *Swar-Bhaskar*, I was lost for words. The writer had buried us all simply by not mentioning Bhimanna's first marriage, his first wife, and us, the children. Bhimanna's marriage had been solemnized in the presence of priests, family, and relatives. The biography is consequently a crass collection of lies. It is surprising that the writer had spent five hours with my grandfather without knowing about us, who had been living for years in Poona. He described 'her' as the wellspring of Bhimanna's inspiration! Obviously the gag in the mouth was cement-hard. The writer could have traced the source of this wellspring down to Badami. Clearly he was constrained to write what he was told to write. Anyway, all my anger has drained out of me now.

Despite the hardships he had to face in his own house, Bhimanna never ceased to explore creatively new vistas of performance. Music gushed from his heart like the waters of the Ganga. Nothing could stall them. I always described him as 'my father made of steel, resonating with music' (*vajra-dehi nadpita*). In later years he mastered the art of hiding his true emotions and adopted a mask suitable for a life dedicated to music. The only way he could give vent to his emotions was through his music into which he poured his heart and soul, illuminating the hearts and souls of his audience. This was especially true when he chose ragas like Todi, Asavari Todi, Jogiya, Marwa, Abhogi, and Bhairavi. His singing was proof of the dictum that all art is a bleeding of the heart. When he sang the bhajan 'Sab paise ke bhai', he was truly speaking of his own mind: the bhajan lay bare his bleeding heart that had suffered the slings and arrows of life. *That* was the wellspring of his moving music.

He stood unaffected, like a rock, in the face of all tribulations. The only occasion when I saw him break down was when Mother passed away. Once, during the last days of his life, he gave up eating food. The nurse told me that the only words he kept repeating were, 'I want go back to Nandi' (Mother). Indeed, a whole book can be written on his last days. It would be a tale of suffering. He became progressively dependent on others following the onset of various ailments. His public appearances became rare. Deep inside, his heart was in flames.

His last performance at the 2007 Sawai Gandharva Sangeet Mahotsav was a pitiable expression of the bleeding heart. His singing was mechanical. It was his swan song dedicated to his devoted audience. The DVD shows him gasping as he said, 'May this festival continue to be held for ever'.

Injections had perforated every inch of his body and medicines had filled his nerves and arteries. He suffered from left frontal meningioma that had paralysed all body control. He had frequent fits. He needed oxygen support at home as he was suffering from hypercarbia (abnormally elevated carbon dioxide levels in the blood). Dipping sodium levels had affected his memory, and he suffered from hallucinations. Catheter and urine bag had sort of become part of his body, often leading to infections. The nurse told me that even in his fits he would often chant the name of Rama. Whenever I met him during those days he would look up at the skies as if to suggest, 'God alone is my help and succour now'. 'Cut my body into pieces. Stab it wherever you wish,' he used to say. In this condition whenever he was dressed up to meet visitors, he seemed to me like a wick whose flame had been extinguished. It was not possible for me to look after him as the vigilance squads prevented it. 'Allow me to take you to my place to nurse you. I am ready any time,' I said to him. He simply gave me a weak smile and remained tongue-tied.

Once he said in Kannada, 'Let these parasites nurse me. They have enjoyed sucking my blood all my life.' That was the truth, plain and simple. But it was again Bhimanna's money that was being used for his treatment. No one else had earned it. The 'others' had enough and more to squander as royalties and awards kept flowing in. He was the proverbial goose that was laying eggs of gold. The parasites were living happily on those eggs.

He lay like Bhishma of the Mahabharata, who slept on a bed of arrows in the battlefield. Once you accept a role you have to play it, willingly or unwillingly, till the very end. That was his plight. What bad luck for this man! He was the emperor of music, but lived like a slave. He was made to beg even for his favourite paan and tobacco. His earnings were an endless booty for the scroungers, and the world was allowed to see only the tinsel. They were often heard wailing, 'All his life this sick man is giving us no end of trouble'. That was the final defeat of a man who had magnanimously distributed blank cheques of happiness among them. How ironical that such a tuneful titan should have such an out-of-tune existence!

At the same time 'new' maestros suddenly began to shoot to fame, catapulted by media fathers. Media hype became the order of the day. Most of those Page 3 stars had no dimensions. 'Designer' Gandharvas emerged with ease as the new icons. It was the other way round now: Nero burnt and Rome sang!

Bhimanna's music has become an inseparable part of my being. I believe that all great music is an expression of deep emotions without which it remains only as a grammatical discipline. Meditation, contemplation, and riyaz are the wellspring of great music; it is not a mere string of notes. Music devoid of emotion is music learnt by rote and delivered like a habit. It is the notes that speak the emotion; they have to be alive and vibrant. There are performers who sing without knowing what makes great music. They are like the proverbial pandit in a sinking boat: well versed in the theory of swimming, but without even having once entered water.

Sensitive ears and infinite patience make a good listener. He is like the *chatak* bird that waits with its beak open for raindrops. Then the music seeps into the soul in a moment of self-realization. This is equivalent to the highest yogic trance, a musical nirvana experience. It stirs the listener's inner being and keeps vibrating in his memory. That is what I experienced while listening to Bhimanna singing. That was what P.B. Shelley meant when he wrote 'Music, when soft voices die,/ Vibrates in the memory.'

It is timeless and takes you to the stars. That was Bhimanna's music.

There can be no parallel to the energy he emitted while performing. It was enough and more to send a Boeing plane around the world. He deserved a Ramon Magsaysay Award or a Nobel Prize. When he was awarded the Bharat Ratna he was asked how he felt about it. He coolly said, 'Nothing!' What was a worldly award to one who had already received a divine one? He was born with music in his every heartbeat. The world looks upon such people with wide-eyed admiration. There are others, marauding plunderers, who take them for Ali Baba's cave, to be looted!

Someone once said to me that Anna entered the state of samadhi (trance) whenever he performed. I told him off; it was not only Anna, but his listeners, too, who shared the experience. 'Try, if you can,' I added.

Bhimanna breathed his last on 24 January 2011. I had missed an opportunity to seek his blessings on my birthday earlier on 26 July. One day when I met him and touched his feet with a request to bless me, he said, 'I did that yesterday'. I was scared that he was losing track of time. 'Bless me in the traditional style,' I insisted and helped him lift his hand to touch my head. Only then was my mind at peace. Well, I believe in such rituals, call them whatever you like! Even now I believe that wherever he may be he blesses me in every moment.

I have crossed seventy and am blessed with a joint family consisting of my wife, two sons, their wives, three grandchildren and, yes, our pet dog Bhurya. We share and care equally. Through hard work I have earned money that had been denied to me in my childhood. I continue to be a water diviner, helping people get water for their lands. Several farms flourish, buildings stand, and people feed on the water I have divined by digging their wells. Seeing others prosper is an unceasing joy for me.

Savitribai Phule Pune University has established a chair in honour of Bhimanna. Hostels for boys and girls on the campus are fed with a continuous water supply from the wells I have divined for them. I have a profound sense of fulfilment. Bhimanna had once quipped, 'I earn from music; he from water!' I had retorted, 'Floods of money from music for *them*; only a few drops for me after breaking rocks!' He had only smiled.

Both music maker and water diviner serve humanity. One quenches the thirst of the heart, the other, of the body. Bhimanna always acknowledged the debt he owed to society and, like the great Bal Gandharva he, too, regarded his audience as his parents. Whenever the need was felt, he gave away in large measures to the needy. Once on his way to Jalandhar he stopped at a wayside restaurant owned by one of his fans. The man requested a souvenir—a piece of cloth—and Bhimanna opened his bag, took out all his shirts, and handed them over to the man.

Bhimanna often helped people incognito, that is, when he was not being watched by 'his people'. One day my wife took an autorickshaw from Poona city to our home in suburban Dhayari and began to explain the exact address to the driver. The man said, 'I have heard that Pandit Bhimsen Joshi's son has a house in the same area. Do you know him?' My wife said, 'That is our house!' When my wife tried to pay him he refused to accept the fare, touched my wife's feet, and said, 'I have reached this stage of my life because of Panditji's grace. I cannot accept any money.' And he left!

Once after his physiotherapy session was over, the nurse asked Bhimanna whether he wanted anything else. He snapped, 'Get lost!' I was surprised and asked him why he was curt to the lady who was so caring towards him. He asked in return,

'How does love matter in life?' It was a suggestive answer. It exposed his heart which had been stabbed and wounded by those crafty parasites whom he had supported and fed for years on end. Great artists are often duped like this. 'Fie on't', as Hamlet said, referring to the world. And that is what Bhimanna meant.

The Sun Sets on Hindustani Vocal Classical Music:
31 December 2010 to 24 January 2011

I rushed to Sahyadri Hospital on learning that Bhimanna had been admitted there. His appearance told me that there was little hope now. He had been put on the ventilator and was in a coma. I kept checking on his condition from time to time; that was the only option left for us. Though the doctors were vigilant he had made his decision.

He regained consciousness on the seventh day. 'I am Raghu,' I said. He nodded in acknowledgement. Then I chanted his favourite mantra 'Shree Rama jai Rama jai jai Rama' and also the Sanskrit prayer to Raghavendra Swami *'Poojyaya Raghavendraya satya dharma ratayacha'* (Pray to Raghavendra Swami and follow the religion of truth). I touched his head and he responded. Then I said, 'Bhimanna, the new year has started. Get well quickly and come back.' He shook his head in disagreement. And I knew it. He seemed like someone from a different world, waiting for his last ride to arrive!

After about eight days when I called to get an update on Bhimanna's health, a doctor answered angrily, 'How do I know that you are his son? Any Tom, Dick, or Harry can inquire and then spread rumours. I cannot tell you.' I lost my temper and snapped back. 'You had no difficulty talking to me during the last eight days. What's wrong with you now? Do I have to sing to prove that I am his son?' 'All right,' he said and disconnected the line.

I was furious that even in my sixties I had to face such humiliation. I knew well who could be stage-managing this drama. A friend of mine advised me to speak to Dr Charu Apte, the chief doctor there. He kindly asked his wife, the hospital administrator, to keep me briefed on Bhimanna's condition with the proviso to keep things confidential. I had circumvented the stratagem of the wily foxes.

The next time I went to the hospital the people there apologized for the harsh words. I learnt that the chief had given a piece of his mind to his assistants. But Bhimanna was sinking....

One day the doctor said to me, 'It is time to make a decision now. How long should we continue to torture him?' I expressed my inability to decide and came out. I saw the 'young prince' standing there. When I repeated the doctor's view this youngster said, 'There are better doctors than him. They will decide.'

Rumours began to make the rounds now. I received a call asking, 'Is Anna no more?' 'I saw him just a while ago; he is stable,' I told the caller. My mind was pulled between two options: soon, Anna may be no more; on the other hand, he was suffering. I had mental pictures of a bedridden Bhimanna. Oh God, give him peace and comfort!

The next morning Dr Atul Joshi called me to tell me that Anna had just passed away. 'Exactly when?' I asked. 'At five past eight'. The body was taken to his house. I broke down into profuse tears. My whole house sank in grief. The telephone would not stop ringing. I started with my elder son Rahul for Bhimanna's house. My younger son Atul was in Delhi.

On reaching there I was moved to see my revered father's lifeless body. It was disturbing to see how crowded the room was. The windows and shutters were closed and there was darkness all around. I had the windows opened and switched on the lights. All the chairs were already occupied by the relatives of the 'other' family. Bhimanna's admirers had to jostle through a narrow space in order to lay flowers at his feet.

My brother and I sat down close by. Bhimanna lay—he looked as if he was a package on consignment—on a shabby bedsheet on the floor. Some of the people in the house were actually crossing over his body, wearing chappals. Reporters and cameramen from various TV channels were milling around in the front yard. Whenever a VIP arrived the house people rushed out to be seen by their side. As quickly as bouquets and garlands were being placed on Bhimanna a burly fellow was taking them off and hurling them out of the window. He was also shouting, 'Move out ... don't crowd here....'

My heart was in agony seeing that after life's fitful fever, even in his death this great man was not allowed to sleep well. A small canopy in the front yard would have been a convenient arrangement for people to flock around and pay their homage. Matters were being rushed through. After the chief minister of Karnataka had paid his tribute the body was placed in an ambulance. We, too, pushed our way in. The 'young prince' was already sitting inside, along with a student of Bhimanna. A hefty student from Bangalore also entered and made the place even more congested.

What a beggarly funeral! A word would have been enough for Bhimanna's admirers to arrange for an open wagon, properly decked and with varkaris singing his favourite bhajans on the last journey of this devotee of Lord Vitthal. Small minds think small.

Someone in the crowd said, 'Just a mention and people would have piled up sandalwood for the cremation'. Even the Karnataka government would have given sandalwood for this Karnataka Ratna, some others felt.

I saw Bhimanna's younger brother Vyankanna and his family in the crowds that were surging uncontrollably every moment. Bhimanna lay wrapped in the national tricolour on a stretcher and we had to wait long for a central minister to arrive. I remembered that his younger brother, Madhukaka, a wing commander in the Air Force, had been wrapped similarly in the national flag.

People were offering their tributes over the mike of the police van. It was clear that the media father, the one who handled media dealings for the 'other' family, was controlling the announcements. The president had sent his condolence addressed to the 'young prince'. This, too, was stage-managed and mentioned particularly on the mike. But was it only the blood relations who felt bereaved? The entire world of music lovers was in tears. However, the hungry media have no sense of shame or propriety anytime, anywhere.

Finally rifles were pointed to the skies and Bhimanna was given a twenty-five gun salute. The crowd surged forward. Bhimanna had wanted me to perform the last rites, and the media father reminded me of that. I could see a crooked smile on his face ridiculing me. He went close to the priest, who was waiting for me, and whispered in his ears to 'speed up' and to 'wind up'. I was boiling with anger and wished my son Rahul, too, was there to handle this creature.

The Joshi traditions brook no shortcuts in religious rites. My maternal aunt Shamakka had explained all the death rites to my uncle when Grandfather Guracharya had passed away. Accordingly, the dead body had to be washed and offered tulsi leaves before cremation. Reporters and media people were shunted out. I made it a point to remind the priest to say all the mantras without any shortcuts. He agreed, though members of the 'other' family seemed reluctant to participate.

Finally Bhimanna's body was moved to the electric crematorium. I was stunned to see all the womenfolk of the 'other' family there. There is no sanction for womenfolk of the Joshi clan to be present at a cremation. But, well, they did not belong to the Joshi clan and they did not consider it a sacrilege.

I told the 'young prince' that Bhimanna's ashes were to be collected from the crematorium and immersed in the river at Alandi near Poona. The next morning we were all there— my sons, Atul and Rahul, my brother Anand, and Bhimanna's sons-in-law. When I reminded the 'young prince' about it he snapped back, 'Hasn't the driver come? I'll send someone else.' Eventually I collected the ashes. For a moment I was paralysed as I realized that they were the remains of my father who had charmed the whole world with his music. I put tulsi leaves and white roses on the ashes, left half of them for the 'young prince', and went to Alandi for the final immersion. The next day the newspapers announced that 'they' had immersed the remains elsewhere! However, those who knew the facts telephoned me to express satisfaction that it was I who had performed the last rites and immersed the remains at Alandi.

The next day I got up, sat in front of my family gods, and wrote an obituary, 'Bhimanna, You Will Never Forsake Us'. It appeared in *Daily Sakal* under a changed title and heavily edited. Certain facts had been excised. Even so I received several calls congratulating me on my honest expression. Ramakantkaka, who had come all the way from Dharwad, liked my article, and he translated it into Kannada for *Samyukta Karnataka*. Eminent journalist Sugata Raju translated it into English for e-Outlook and it got wide circulation and many hits all over the world.

After thirteen days we went to Omkareshwar, the place where several rites are traditionally performed. One of them is the offering of rice balls to crows. Liberation or salvation of the soul of the deceased is guaranteed if a crow eats the rice ball! It posed no problem for Bhimanna as a crow

209

immediately touched the rice ball. I was suddenly reminded how he sometimes indulged in quibbles. He would have told the crows: do it melodiously please; I am Bhimsen, the Hindustani classical vocalist!

The chief priest at Mantralayam math had wished the prayers to be said at Raghavendra Swami math in Poona. Nobody from the 'other' family attended it. It was given out that they had no time for such things. Subsequently there was a flood of memorial meetings, some genuine with unquestionable involvement and some others for newspaper publicity. A condolence meeting was reported to have been held in Paris. Articles appeared in the *New York Times* and the *Guardian*. I became aware for the first time in my life that my father was loved beyond the borders of the country. Hindustani classical music has a history of barely 300 years, but Bhimanna had established a record for the highest number of concerts in the world. Seldom has any other vocalist of classical music enjoyed so much popularity in life. People described him as a *deep-sthambh* (lighthouse) of Hindustani classical music or an emperor of concerts. Tributes were showered on him in the remotest possible villages of India. I had been to only a few of these tributes.

Soon after Bhimanna passed away a bolt from the blue hit me—Bhimanna's will! The 'other' family dug out some paper they called Bhimanna's will. It was read out at his bungalow, Kalashree, when all the members of the house and some hangers-on were present. I wondered what the will said. First of all it declared that the earlier will stood null and void. A cock-and-bull story had been fabricated with particulars of money given to us. It also declared that all of Bhimanna's earnings and possessions in cash and kind as well as the proceeds from royalties in future were the property of the 'other' family only. It also sullied Mother's memory with the allegation that Bhimanna had lived with her only for a few months.

For years Bhimanna had been unable to speak properly, but the will contained umpteen figurative expressions as having been uttered by him. The whole document was a model of crass and outright falsehood. It was not *his* will, but the will of a pack of wolves. I told them, 'Our father had already been hijacked. What else can this contain?' And I left. It was a flagrant plot to capture and control the Arya Sangeet Prasarak Mandal Trust and the Sawai Gandharva Sangeet Mahotsav rights. I resolved to fight it so that truth could prevail. The eminent Kannada writer S.L. Bhyrappa had once visited Poona and concluded a discourse with the great tenet, 'Truth alone wins ultimately'. I asked him, 'Is it really true? If so, why does it take so long to win, and why does it happen only at the end of everything?' He simply smiled.

❧

Bhimanna's life in his own home had been an endless chain of humiliations. He once said to an acquaintance, 'I am like a pair of shoes. Put them on when you need them, throw them away when no longer needed.' His neighbour told me, 'He was deprived even of a simple dish of fried poha. We often gave him this favourite dish of his. He would, then, give my children chocolates with a warning not to mention it to anyone.'

Mohan Nadkarni's book *Bhimsen Joshi: A Biography* also records this situation. It says, 'Although he lived there, he did not belong there. He was very lonely. He would discuss only

211

music with me. His personal life was under a big lock and key.' Never in my life did he have a bad word to say against Mother or against us. He left that part to the people at 'home', who never ceased from declaring that we were evil. What did they mean? That we were evil because Bhimanna had married our mother and fathered us?

What is this life after all if not simply a vortex of existence in which we flounder and eventually get swept away? Bhimanna kept turning in the vortex of popularity and performances. No one, not even he himself, could see the ordinary human being in him. Sometimes he would be in a confessional mood and tell his student Madhav Gudi (who told me so), 'I am the cause of the entire disaster. But it can't be helped now.'

Whenever he sang Bhairavi and saw me sitting in front of him, he recognized the beggar in me asking for his grace. But he never gave me any alms. It was I who picked up whatever crumbs I could from him. I believe that 'to sing' means to get one's battery charged with the guru's melodious notes and reproduce them whenever one wishes to perform. Then one develops one's own skills, one's own identity. My fate resembled that of Eklavya of the Mahabharata who was denied training by Guru Dronacharya. But Eklavya practised and gained extreme skill in archery. I couldn't. But, then, Guru Dronacharya had at least another ambidextrous disciple in Arjun. Who was Bhimanna's Arjun? It is all an infinite mystery there. And I would say this about those ones who claim to be his true disciples, 'Forgive them, my lord, for they know not what they sing'. Bimanna was painfully aware of the vacuum ahead of him as no disciple seemed to be up to the mark to continue his great tradition.

Bhimanna's guru, Sawai Gandharva, had hurled a steel nutcracker at him because he was not singing a note correctly.

Bhimanna carried the scar on his forehead where the object had hit him. That was how teachers were back then. But it was like obtaining gold out of ordinary metal only after putting it in a furnace. The riyaz would continue until the vocal cords produced the exact note. Unlike today disciples never earned a word of praise from their gurus, who had no desire to send out croaking frogs. Once when Bhimanna was listening to an ugly performance by a student he shouted, 'Hit him with a tanpura!' Later this same man began to prefix Pandit to his name! Bhimanna resented it. He also exclaimed, 'If Raghu had been trained....' But, then, spies and watchdogs vigilantly kept Bhimanna from sharing his art with me.

I once reminded him of what Mother had said to him, 'You will cut off all of us without a paisa, we know'. He added insult to our injury by uttering some crudity. But, then, he was suffering from brain tumour. I asked him, 'How is it you always believed only the liars? I am your son. I love you to no end. But have I asked for any money after I started earning independently?'

'No,' he replied.

'I always followed your instructions precisely. Tell me once and for all if I am to see you again.'

He stiffened in his wheelchair, as if struggling to rise, and shouted, 'Did I ever say so? Did I ever say so?'

I knew he loved me dearly and could not think of losing me. Nobody could ever delete his 'Raghu' from his heart. That was enough for me. I put at his feet his favourite fruit—figs—and left.

Once when I touched his feet and sat in front of him, he looked furtively behind him and asked in a hushed voice, 'What do you want?' He feared that someone might be spying on us. He was continuously under watch.

Was his brain tumour caused by such extreme sorrow and humiliation? It is worth researching.

∞∞

When I look back an endless chain of thoughts and memories flash before my mind's eye:

... I fail to understand how I could stand all that pain and suffering ...
... Mother shedding tears ceaselessly ...
... the crisp smell of new shoes brought by Bhimanna for me for the first time ...
... the gifts received during my thread ceremony ...
... the dazzling brass-band players ...
... my teacher, Mr Parchure, asking me to sing 'Hari ka bhed na payo' in class ...
... sitting through several thrilling concerts of Bhimanna's ...
... higher education up to a degree certificate ...
... raga Marwa taught only once by Bhimanna with its haunting notation ...
... my riyaz of those notes ...
... falling in love ...

I remember having walked for miles with my beloved in sheer joy of landing in a job with an appointment letter in hand!

... dreaming of a rosy future ...
... how happy Bhimanna and Mother looked together at my marriage ...
... what a Herculean task it had been for me and my wife to build our house in Dhayari ...
... the first flowers and fruits in our garden ...
... the birth of Rahul and Atul, my sons ...
... struggling, as the eldest, to help my siblings settle in life ...
... my pain at the untimely demise of my two friends ...
... our elation when I started my own business and amassed our first lakh rupees ...

... our first Fiat car, which Bhimanna himself drove all the way to
his house ...
... the death of Mother after a prolonged illness and how thoroughly
shaken Bhimanna was by the loss ... his consoling caress on my back ...
... the birth of my first grandson, Pranav, when we offered flowers made of
gold to Bhimanna who was now a great-grandfather ...
... the unforgettable award of Bharat Ratna for Bhimanna ...
... Bhimanna's agonies, his painful death, the last Bhairavi ... echoing
in the far off horizons.

It all comes back to me like a movie. There is no end to
memories and there are far too many to note down.

I see my grandchildren Pranav, Urvi, and Amogh growing
as I share a swing with them in our courtyard scented with the
gentle fragrance of akashmogra flowers.

... Where will all of us be fifty years hence...?
... What will these trees be like then...?

Everything will continue to be as it is now even after I am
no more. It is an absorbing daydream.

⟨⟩

There is no way of knowing who composed raga Bhairavi.
Made of soft notes, it transports one to the ultimate truth.
Bhimanna saw the many faces of this raga in bhajans. He
showed the way to that ultimate truth.

I, the son of a vocal maestro, was never given to greed
or to grabbing others' possessions. Perhaps that stopped me
from becoming a celebrity. But when I close my eyes for a
moment and tune my vocal cords to repeat what he gave
me, I am transported to his world of the ultimate truth,
and I forge a live communication with him. This is my
ultimate fulfilment.

Abdul Karim Khan Sahib is said to have breathed his last while singing raga Darbari after which he lay down to sleep forever. I always prayed for the same end for Bhimanna. Maybe he, too, looked forward to a similar end. But destiny had a different plan for him. Love of one's parents, love of one's wife or beloved, love of one's children are rare gifts. But the love of a singer's son for his father's music has no parallel for me. It is an ever-flowing stream of fresh water in my life. The sum total of my life is found when I recall Bhimanna's favourite bhajan '*Mat kar moh tu, Haribhajan ko maan re*' (Rise above temptation, recite Haribhajan). This music is the be-all and the end-all of my life. This is the writing of my destiny as the progeny of a vocal legend. Remember how Bhimanna would rest peacefully on the lower note—the lower shadja of Bhairavi. Stable and steady, to perfection. The total fulfilment for me would be to settle thus, tuneful and melodious.

Somewhere in a remote village, working at the drilling at the bottom of a well, as the clouds of dust covered me all over, I would attune myself with the buzzing sound of the compressor, as if it were singing a song sung by Bhimanna. It was like the liberation of the soul when the waters gushed out of the rock, cleaning everything that was soiled. All the layers of suffering of life would then be washed away by the constant gush of life, evoking cries of joy from the onlookers. The waters had a life-giving force for several lives around. The bliss that I got from Bhimanna's singing was the same as the bliss that gushed from those waters.

I often dream a dream...

... Bhimanna is performing and I am sitting behind him, accompanying him on the tanpura.

... As he pauses, he gives me a cue to try a note.
... His eyes shower beams of affection on me ...

I wake up with the same notes of the same raga on my lips. May God grant me such a tuneful life next time ... please ... make me not the forsaken son.

~

1. Shankar Abhyankar, *Swar-Bhaskar* (Kolhapur: Ajab Pustakalaya, 1983).

Raghavendra Bhimsen Joshi is the eldest son of Hindustani classical vocal maestro Bharat Ratna Bhimsen Joshi. He witnessed his whole life from close quarters with great affection and respect and knew all his emotional compulsions. He is a science graduate from the University of Pune. He served in the defence production for fifteen years and subsequently resigned to start his own business of borewell drilling. He has published many articles in Marathi newspapers, magazines, and books. This book is the English translation of his Marathi autobiography *Ganaryache Por* (2013).

Shirish Chindhade, the former principal of M.U. College of Commerce, Pimpri, Pune, has a PhD in Indian English poetry. He has published several articles (in English and Marathi) on literary and non-literary topics and written about twenty books of diverse interests, including *Mentoring Colleges for Assessment and Accreditation* (co-authored; 2016), *Dimensions of Research in Literature* (2014), *Assessment and Accreditation as NAAC Peer Teams See It* (2013), *Innovative Practices and Case Studies in Higher Education* (2013), *Approved Voices* (2006), and *Five Indian English Poets* (1996). He translates from and into Marathi and English, and has translated Albert Camus's novel *The Outsider* into Marathi (1974). Presently he lives in Pune.